D0572721

I DEDICATE THIS TO MY MUM,
WHO INSPIRED ME TO COOK
FROM AN EARLY AGE.

FULL ON IRISH

CREATIVE CONTEMPORARY COOKING

KEVIN DUNDON

EPICURE PRESS

P.O. Box 6173, Dublin 13.

ISBN 1-903164-22-2

Publishing Editor: Georgina Campbell

Contributing Editor: Orla Broderick

Producers Editor: Biddy White Lennon

Home Economist: Sharon Hearne

US Conversions: Charlotte Coleman-Smith

Design: Helen Hayes, White or Cream, Dublin

Photography: Alan Murphy

Author Acknowledgements

To all the team at Dunbrody Country House who have been enthusiastic guinea pigs to the successes and failures of my culinary experiments and in particular my Main Man and talented chef - Phelim Byrne.

To my wife Catherine who will be pleased to sit down to dinner in peace without having me ask "well, what do you think?" before being given the chance to taste the first mouthful.

To my daughters Emily and Sophie who have chomped through the pages of this book with gusto and are learning to be discerning young tasters.

To Orla Broderick for managing to keep me focused.

To Sharon Hearne for her stylish interpretation of the recipes.

To Alan Murphy who has brought my food alive with his superb photography.

To Helen Hayes for her innovative and creative designs.

To Georgina Campbell for her tireless support and enthusiasm.

And finally to Martine Carter, my agent, and Mary Jones, my publicist, for their indefatigable commitment to the project.

It's been a great pleasure to know and work with each one of you. Thank You.

Kevin Dundon,
Dunbrody Country House,
October, 2005

Printed and bound in Italy

Contents

Introduction

My passion for food began at a very early age. My mother and grandmother are both wonderful cooks, giving me the inspiration to celebrate all that is best in Irish food, and a growing love for its special nature.

In these pages, we take you on a gourmet tour of today's Irish cooking, looking at traditional dishes, and how they can be given a gentle facelift. The result is a collection of recipes which will offer great ideas for your family dinners, and meals with friends.

We are going to source ingredients locally, and introduce you to some of County Wexford's best producers, bringing you through the heart-warming story behind our fantastic farmhouse cheeses, and the superb produce from land and sea throughout Ireland.

The revival of Irish farmhouse cheese-making has been the greatest success story of Ireland's artisan food culture in recent years, and has encouraged many other small producers to succeed in their own areas of speciality. Our cheeses are complex and wild, and this gives them that special edge. Created by innovative and dedicated people with pride and respect for their craft, it makes me very proud that they can stand comparison with any cheese worldwide.

Through our cheeses, you can taste the salty winds of the Atlantic Ocean … the softness of the rolling Wexford hills … the rugged Cork and Kerry coastline – the best Irish cheeses are an expressive reflection of their origins. With their individuality and quality, they have earned the respect of the international food community. We will guide you in appreciating the range of farmhouse cheeses being produced in Ireland, and give an insight into the remarkable specialists behind a craft that is traditional yet also demonstrates vividly the direction that the best of contemporay Irish food is now taking. A personal favourite is *Mine Gabhar* goat's cheese from Blackwater on County Wexford's pasture-rich east coast - you'll find the story in this book.

The real joy of cooking for me is that I can source virtually all of the ingredients that we use at Dunbrody Country House within the county of Wexford, much of it from our own gardens and from neighbouring farms. I am often asked if everything we use in our kitchens is organic – and, although our own kitchen gardens are organic, my answer is that there is no point choosing to use imported organic produce, which may have travelled many thousands of miles before arriving in Ireland, when there are so many excellent traditional producers nearby, allowing fresh seasonal produce to be harvested on a daily basis and brought directly to the kitchen. This freshness going straight to the plate makes the flavours simply unbeatable.

Another 'straight to plate' ingredient is our wide choice of fish. Plump and juicy scallops from Kilmore Quay, cockles and mussels from Baginbun Bay, wild salmon from the Waterford estuary - and there's also swordfish, tuna and sea bass landed regularly in our local harbour at Duncannon. Similarly, our meats come from trusted butchers, and I am confident in the knowledge that I know the farmers who produce the food that we serve, as well as the butchers who supply us.

The underlying theme of this book is my belief in food which is clean, fresh and creative - using only the best of ingredients in accordance with the seasons. The recipes are simple to follow, yet with great results. For the experienced gourmet and the enthusiastic home cook alike, I hope this will be seen as a kitchen guidebook, a one-stop shop which shows you the way from the everyday to the special occasion, all year round.

Dunbrody, our beloved place, is the heart of it. My wife Catherine and I opened the doors of this restored house in 1997 with the dream of creating a unique venue to celebrate classic and contemporary Irish hospitality in style.

We invite you to share and enjoy our living dream, symbolised by the heron which has always been part of the ancient crest of Dunbrody, and is still with us today.

CASTLETOWN

DUNMORE EAST CO-OP

DUNMORE EAST CO-OP
NO UNAUTHORISED USE
EL: 353-51-383307 FAX: 353-51-383446

BUY MICHAEL

Soups

COLCANNON SOUP WITH CHEESE STRAWS 16

WILD FOREST MUSHROOM CHOWDER 19

KILMORE QUAY CRAB INFUSION 20

TOMATO AND POITÍN SOUP 23

IRISH OAK SMOKED SALMON AND COCKLE SOUP 24

HEARTY IRISH BROTH 27

DUNCANON SEAFOOD CHOWDER 28

ROASTED GOOSE AND CHESTNUT SOUP 31

Soups

BAGINBUN BAY COCKLES

Cockles thrive on estuaries and sandy shores like Baginbun Bay in County Wexford where wild foods have been harvested for centuries. They have a double heart-shaped shell which comes in a variety of shades of brown, yellow, dirty white, pink and even blue. Cockles are plentiful all round the coast of Ireland, if you know where to find them and the trick of gathering them. They bury themselves beneath the sand and have to be gathered at low tide. You can sometimes spot them if you stand near the water's edge and look for small jets of water squirting out of the sand; the cockles are siphoning the water for oxygen.

Digging them out is hard, no matter how fast you dig the faster they will burrow into the sand. When I go on a cockle gathering expedition I use the preferred tool in Ireland, a wooden rake with which I methodically rake the sand a few inches deep, a method I find is usually successful at bringing them to the surface. Get them into a bucket fast or they disappear under the sand again. Once gathered they should be swirled around in water and then soaked in clean sea water, or in salted water, for a few hours to purge themselves. Before cooking, a quick wash under cold running water will get rid of any sand, grit, or mud. The popularity of the cockle in Ireland is celebrated in song *Sweet Molly Malone* who wheeled her wheelbarrow through streets broad and narrow crying "cockles and mussels alive, alive o."

She was selling *cerastoderma edule*, the common cockle, which along with *glossidae cardidiae*, the heart cockle, is common in Europe. Irish cockles are quite small (about 6cm/2^1/$_4$in) and tender and should be alive when you begin preparing them for the pot. As for example *Irish oak smoked salmon and cockle soup* (page 24).

Many varieties of edible bivalves from different parts of the world are called cockles. On the American side of the Atlantic you'll find the Iceland cockle (which ranges from Greenland to Massachusetts) and the much larger Atlantic cockle, a southerly species rare north of Florida. On the Pacific coast quite a few so-called cockles are really their first cousins the clams but can be used in place of cockles quite successfully; but there is one really good one called the basket cockle.

I SERVE THIS SOUP WITH MY MORE-ISH CHEESE STRAWS, WHICH ARE A FANTASTIC CANAPÉ, PERFECT TO KICK-START ANY DINNER PARTY. THEY CAN BE MADE UP TO THREE DAYS IN ADVANCE AND STORED IN AN AIRTIGHT CONTAINER AT ROOM TEMPERATURE. CRISP IN A PREHEATED OVEN AT 200°C/400°F/GAS 6 FOR 2-3 MINUTES BEFORE SERVING.

COLCANNON SOUP *with* CHEESE STRAWS

FOR THE CHEESE STRAWS

175g/6oz sheet ready-rolled puff pastry, thawed if frozen

plain flour, for dusting

50g/2oz Cheddar cheese, finely grated

1 egg yolk beaten with 2 tsp water

FOR THE CRISPY PARMA HAM SHARDS

1 slice Parma ham

FOR THE COLCANNON SOUP

50g/2oz rindless streaky bacon, diced

1 onion, finely chopped

225g/8oz potatoes, diced

1 leek, thinly sliced

150g/5oz Savoy cabbage, thick stalks removed and shredded

700ml/1¼ pints/3 cups kitchen garden vegetable stock (page 168) or water

150ml/¼ pint/⅔ cup cream

25g/1oz/¼ stick butter, diced (at room temperature)

coarse sea salt and freshly ground black pepper

Serves 4-6

Preheat the oven to 180°C/350°F/Gas 4.

TO MAKE THE CHEESE STRAWS, place the puff pastry on a lightly floured work surface and sprinkle over the Cheddar in an even layer. Fold in half widthways to enclose the cheese layer completely and roll out again to its original size, using a little extra flour if necessary. Brush all over with the beaten egg and place in the fridge for 15 minutes to rest.

Take the chilled cheese pastry and cut it into 10cm/4in lengths, each 1cm/1½in wide. Hold the ends of each strip between your fingers and twist the ends in opposite directions. Arrange the twisted strips on non-stick baking sheets and sprinkle a little salt over each one. Bake for 10 minutes or until crisp and golden brown, then transfer to a wire rack and leave to cool. Serve warm or at room temperature (see introduction above).

TO MAKE THE CRISPY PARMA HAM SHARDS, rip the Parma ham into long thin strips and arrange on a baking sheet lined with greaseproof paper. Bake in the oven for 5 minutes until crispy and then leave to cool.

TO MAKE THE COLCANNON SOUP, heat a large pan and sauté the bacon over a medium to high heat for a couple of minutes until the fat comes out. Stir in the onion, potatoes, leek and cabbage, then cover with a lid and sweat over a medium heat for 10 minutes until well softened but not coloured, stirring occasionally.

Pour the vegetable stock or water into the cabbage mixture and bring to the boil, then season to taste. Stir in the cream and simmer for a few minutes until the soup has a creamy texture.

TO SERVE, remove the soup from the heat and whisk in the butter. It is important not to reboil the soup once the butter has been added or you'll find it will curdle. Ladle the colcannon soup into cappuccino cups or warmed serving bowls and arrange a crispy Parma ham shard and a cheese straw to the side. Serve the remaining cheese straws in a separate dish at the table, or use as a canapé.

WILD FOREST MUSHROOM CHOWDER

FOR A REAL WOW FACTOR SERVE THIS SOUP IN A BROWN SODA BREAD CONTAINER AS SHOWN IN THE PICTURE. PREHEAT THE OVEN TO 180°C/350°F/GAS 4 AND LIGHTLY DUST THE INSIDES OF FOUR HEATPROOF SERVING BOWLS. DIVIDE ONE QUANTITY OF MY BROWN SODA BREAD (PAGE 157) INTO FOUR AND DROP INTO THE BOWLS, THEN BAKE FOR 50 MINUTES TO 1 HOUR UNTIL WELL RISEN AND GOLDEN BROWN. LEAVE TO COOL, THEN CUT OFF THE TOPS AND SCOOP OUT THE INSIDES, LEAVING A LAYER OF BREAD FROM THE CRUST BEFORE LADLING IN THE SOUP TO SERVE.

2 tsp olive oil

125g/4 ½ oz/1 ¼ sticks butter, diced (at room temperature)

150g/5oz onion, finely chopped

1 garlic clove, crushed

550g/1 ¼ lb forest mushrooms, chopped (such as chanterelle, oyster and shiitake)

120ml/4 fl oz/ ½ cup white wine

900ml/1 ½ pints/4 cups kitchen garden vegetable stock (page 168) or water

150ml/ ¼ pint/ ⅔ cup cream

salt and freshly ground black pepper

torn flat-leaf parsley, to garnish

Serves 4–6

Heat a heavy-based pan and add the olive oil and a knob of the butter. Once the butter is foaming, tip in the onion, garlic and mushrooms and cook slowly for 4-5 minutes until tender but not coloured. Take out and reserve some of the mushroom mixture to garnish.

Add the wine to the pan and allow to evaporate until reduced by half, then season to taste. Add the vegetable stock or water, stirring to combine and bring to the boil. Reduce the heat and simmer for 15-20 minutes until slightly reduced and all the flavours have had the chance to infuse.

Stir the cream into the pan and leave to simmer for another few minutes, then transfer to a food processor or liquidiser and whizz to a purée.

TO SERVE, remove the soup from the heat and whisk in the remaining butter. Season to taste and ladle into warmed serving bowls, then garnish with the reserved mushrooms and the torn flat-leaf parsley.

THIS SOUP HAS TO BE THE HEIGHT OF INDULGENCE AND TASTES SUBLIME.
IT MIGHT TAKE A BIT OF EFFORT BUT WILL CERTAINLY IMPRESS YOUR GUESTS.

KILMORE QUAY CRAB INFUSION

550g/1¼ lb cooked crab claws, plus
4 shelled crab claws to garnish

2 tbsp/2½ US tablespoons olive oil

2 tsp clarified butter (page 160)

1 onion, finely chopped

300g/11oz carrots, finely diced

1 garlic clove, thinly sliced

50g/2oz/2½ US tablespoons tomato purée

50ml/2fl oz/¼ cup brandy

400ml/14fl oz/1²⁄₃ cups cream

50g/2oz shallots, finely chopped

1 tbsp/1¼ US tablespoons
chopped fresh coriander

½ lemon, pips removed

50g/2oz/½ stick butter, diced
(at room temperature)

salt and freshly ground black pepper

fresh whole chives, to garnish

white bread rolls, to serve
(page 155)

Serves 4-6

Crack the crab claws and remove all of the meat, picking over it carefully – you'll need about 300g/11oz in total. Place in a bowl, cover with cling film and chill until needed. Reserve the crab shells.

Heat a large heavy-based pan with half of the olive oil. Add the clarified butter and then tip in the onion, carrots and garlic. Sauté for a few minutes, then add the reserved crab shells and the tomato purée. Season generously with pepper and continue to cook for 3-4 minutes, stirring constantly.

Pour the brandy into the pan and allow to cook off for a minute or so. Pour in 1 litre/1³⁄₄ pints/4¹⁄₂ cups of water and bring to the boil, then reduce the heat and simmer for 30 minutes until well flavoured and slightly reduced.

Remove the pan from the heat and strain the liquid through a fine sieve into a clean pan, then simmer until reduced by half. Pour in the cream and simmer for another 5 minutes. Season to taste and keep warm or leave to cool and reheat as required.

Heat a sauté pan. Add the remaining olive oil and then tip in the shallots. Sauté for a minute or two and then stir in the reserved white crab meat and the coriander. Continue to sauté for a minute or so until heated through, then season to taste and add a squeeze of lemon juice.

TO SERVE, remove the soup from the heat and whisk in the butter until just combined. Place a 5cm/2in cooking ring that is 5cm/2in deep, in the centre of each warmed wide-rimmed serving bowl and fill with the crab mixture. Carefully remove the ring and garnish each one with a crab claw, then ladle the soup around it. Finish with the whole chives and serve with some of the bread rolls on the side.

TOMATO AND POITÍN SOUP

THIS IS ONE OF MY FAVOURITE 'EMPTY LARDER' RECIPES THAT REQUIRES LITTLE PREPARATION AND IS QUICKLY COOKED. POITIN IS A TRADITIONAL IRISH SPIRIT THAT IS MADE FROM POTATOES. IT IS NOW SOLD UNDER A NUMBER OF COMMERCIAL BRANDS AND REALLY DOES HAVE A UNIQUE FLAVOUR. LOOK OUT FOR IT IN DUTY FREE THE NEXT TIME YOU ARE PASSING THROUGH - OR GIN IS A GOOD ALTERNATIVE.

2 tbsp/2 ½ US tablespoons olive oil

1 small onion, finely chopped

2 garlic cloves, finely chopped

1kg/2 ¼ lb ripe plum tomatoes, halved

50ml/2fl oz/ ¼ cup poitín or gin

700ml/1 ¼ pints/3 cups kitchen garden vegetable stock (page 168) or water

pinch light muscovado sugar (optional)

225ml/8fl oz/1 cup cream

salt and freshly ground black pepper

crème fraîche and snipped fresh chives, to garnish

Serves 4-6

Heat the olive oil in a pan over a medium-high heat. Add the onion and garlic and sauté for a few minutes until golden. Add the tomatoes and continue to sauté for another 5 minutes or so until well heated through and just beginning to break down.

Pour the poitín or gin into the pan and allow to reduce by half, stirring occasionally. Stir in the vegetable stock or water and allow to reduce by half again. Blitz with a hand blender to a smooth purée. Season to taste and add the sugar if you think the soup needs it.

TO SERVE, add the cream to the soup and allow to warm through. Season to taste and ladle into warmed serving bowls. Garnish each bowl with a small dollop of crème fraîche and a sprinkling of chives.

IRISH OAK SMOKED SALMON AND COCKLE SOUP

VERY STYLISH, VERY EASY TO MAKE AND VERY DELICIOUS: THE PERFECT SOUP! IT REALLY HAS A DELICATE FLAVOUR AND SIGNIFIES THE BEST OF WHAT THE SEA AND GARDEN HAVE TO OFFER IN JUNE. COCKLES ARE OFTEN SOLD COOKED BUT IF YOU CAN GET FRESH ONES SIMPLY ADD THE WHOLE SHELLS IN WITH THE VEGETABLES AND CONTINUE AS DESCRIBED BELOW.

2 tsp olive oil

1 onion, finely chopped

1 garlic clove, crushed

200g/7oz asparagus tips, trimmed and chopped

splash white wine

500ml/18fl oz/2 1/4 cups kitchen garden vegetable stock (page 168) or water

pinch saffron strands

125g/4 1/2 oz freshly cooked cockle meat (see introduction above)

125g/4 1/2 oz smoked salmon slices, cut into julienne (long thin strips)

salt and freshly ground black pepper

Serves 4-6

Heat a heavy-based pan and add the olive oil. Tip in the onion, garlic and asparagus, stirring to combine. Cook gently for 4-5 minutes without colouring, stirring occasionally. Pour in the white wine and allow to bubble down and evaporate. Season to taste.

Pour the vegetable stock or water into the pan and add the saffron. Bring to the boil, then reduce the heat and simmer for about 5 minutes, until the asparagus is completely tender and the flavours have infused. Stir in the cockle meat and smoked salmon and allow to just warm through.

TO SERVE, season to taste and ladle into warmed serving glasses or bowls.

HEARTY IRISH BROTH

THIS IS THE SORT OF SOUP THAT PLEADS TO BE EATEN WHEN YOU ARE FEELING TIRED AND JADED. SERVE IT WITH SOME WARM CRUSTY BREAD SLATHERED WITH BUTTER – DELICIOUS! I LIKE TO MAKE IT IN THE AUTUMN WHEN PLUM TOMATOES ARE AT THEIR BEST AND IN AMPLE SUPPLY. THE OTHER VEGETABLES ARE ALL GROWN IN OUR KITCHEN GARDEN.

2 tbsp/2½ US tablespoons olive oil

1 onion, chopped

½ green cabbage, thick stalks removed and shredded

1 leek, thinly sliced

2 potatoes, diced

8 ripe plum tomatoes, diced

120ml/4fl oz/½ cup dry white wine

1 litre/1¾ pints/4½ cups kitchen garden vegetable stock (page 168) or water

salt and freshly ground black pepper

fresh flat-leaf parsley sprigs, to garnish

white bread rolls, to serve (page 155)

Serves 4–6

Heat the olive oil in a large pan and add the onion, cabbage, leek and potatoes, stirring to combine. Cover with a lid and sweat over a medium heat for about 5 minutes until softened but not coloured.

Add the tomatoes to the pan, season to taste and allow to cook for a couple of minutes. Pour in the wine and allow to reduce by half, then add the stock or water and bring to the boil. Reduce the heat and leave to simmer for 15 minutes until all of the vegetables are completely tender and the liquid has slightly reduced and thickened. Season to taste.

TO SERVE, ladle the soup into warmed serving bowls and garnish with the parsley.

DUNCANNON SEAFOOD CHOWDER

A BOWL OF SOUP MUST BE ONE OF THE MOST WELCOMING FOODS KNOWN TO MAN. THIS SEAFOOD CHOWDER ALWAYS GOES DOWN WELL BUT PARTICULARLY WHEN IT IS BITTERLY COLD OUTSIDE. IT IS JUST SO RICH AND TASTY WITH THE MOST WONDERFUL INFUSION OF SHELLFISH, FRESH AND SMOKED FISH. THE SECRET OF THIS SOUP IS NOT TO OVERCOOK THE FISH, SO BEAR IN MIND THAT EVERYTHING CONTINUES TO COOK EVEN AFTER IT IS TAKEN OFF THE HEAT.

25g/1oz/¼ stick butter

1 small onion, diced

1 leek, diced

1 small carrot, diced

1 potato, cubed

50g/2oz smoked salmon slices, cut into julienne (long thin strips)

120ml/4fl oz/½ cup dry white wine

450ml/¾ pint/2 cups fennel scented fish stock (page 167) or water

225g/8oz mixed fresh fish fillets, skinned and cut into bite-sized pieces (such as cod, haddock, hake and salmon)

175g/6oz raw Dublin Bay prawns and mussels, scrubbed clean

1 tbsp/1¼ US tablespoons chopped fresh flat-leaf parsley

175ml/6fl oz/¾ cup cream

salt and freshly ground black pepper

Serves 4-6

Heat a large pan over a medium heat. Add the butter and when it is foaming, tip in the onion, leek, carrot, potato and smoked salmon. Sauté for 2-3 minutes until softened.

Pour the wine into the pan and allow to bubble down and reduce by half. Add the fish stock or water and bring to a simmer, then add the fresh fish and shellfish.

Return the pan to a simmer and add the parsley and cream, then season to taste. Cover with a lid and simmer gently for another 2-3 minutes until the fish and prawns are tender and all of the mussels have opened; discard any that do not.

TO SERVE, ladle the chowder into warmed serving bowls, piling plenty of the fish and shellfish into the centre of each one and garnish with chopped parsley.

ROASTED GOOSE AND CHESTNUT SOUP

GOOSE IS STILL VERY MUCH A SEASONAL BIRD AND DOES NOT USUALLY APPEAR ON OUR SHELVES BEFORE AUTUMN. AN EARLY SEASON GOOSE WEIGHS APPROXIMATELY 4.5KG/10LB, WHICH IS A GOOD SIZE FOR ROASTING FOR SUNDAY LUNCH OR A DINNER PARTY. THE LEFTOVERS WILL SUIT THIS SOUP PERFECTLY AND WOULD FREEZE WELL. ALTERNATIVELY USE SOME DUCK CONFIT, WHICH ALSO WILL GIVE AN EXCELLENT RESULT. THE THAI GREEN CURRY PASTE MAY SEEM LIKE AN UNEXPECTED INGREDIENT BUT IT REALLY COMPLEMENTS THE FLAVOUR OF THE GOOSE.

2 tbsp/2½ US tablespoons sunflower oil

1 onion, finely chopped

1 garlic clove, crushed

2 tbsp/2½ US tablespoons Thai green curry paste

50g/2oz cooked goose meat, chopped, plus extra to garnish (see introduction above)

50g/2oz cooked chestnuts, chopped (vacuum-packed or from a can is fine)

400g/14oz head broccoli, trimmed and roughly chopped

900ml/1½ pints/4 cups kitchen garden vegetable stock (page 168) or water

150ml/¼ pint/⅔ cup cream

salt and freshly ground pepper

Serves 4–6

Heat the oil in a heavy-based pan. Add the onion, garlic, Thai green curry paste, goose meat, chestnuts and broccoli and cook slowly for 4-5 minutes without colouring, stirring occasionally.

Pour the stock or water into the pan and allow to simmer for 10-15 minutes until the broccoli is completely tender but still retaining its colour, and all of the flavours have had time to infuse.

Transfer the soup to a food processor or liquidiser or use a hand blender and whizz until blended.

TO SERVE, stir the cream into the soup and allow to warm through. Season to taste and then ladle into warmed serving bowls. Garnish each one with a little cooked goose meat.

FANCY FUNGI

I love cooking with wild mushrooms. Many edible, exotic mushrooms grow wild in the woodlands of Ireland but the seasonal availability of these wild mushrooms is limited, the most favoured ones can also be elusive, making mushroom hunting time-consuming. I was delighted to discover two bright young men Nicky Dempsey and Nick George had caught the mushroom bug in Crossabeg just a few miles down the road from Dunbrody. Under the catchy name *Fancy Fungi* they grow a variety of mushrooms usually available only from the wild. They provide a regular supply of exotic gourmet fungi, full of flavour and beautiful to look at: golden and grey oyster mushrooms, shitake and portabello, perfect for my *Wild forest mushroom chowder* (page 19). They also experiment with new varieties to see how they will thrive in their growing conditions.

They aim to grow mushrooms in conditions as close to nature as possible. They do everything from scratch, a harder task than you might imagine. Exotic mushrooms are finicky and don't grow on regular mushroom compost. Nicky and Nick make up their own compost so that the growing medium is as close as possible to what the mushroom spawn would encounter in the wild. The compost is packed into black bags, mixed with spawn, and placed in lofty, well-insulated growing sheds. Carefully regulated heat, light, and humidity levels are important to bring the mushrooms on. Nick explains that they must be patient and flexible. The mushrooms start growing when they feel like it and pickers have to be ready to spring into action whenever they choose to flush. Wild exotic mushrooms tend to have big open gills and take in moisture quickly; so, unlike ordinary cultivated mushrooms, their shelf-life is short. Getting them quickly to the customer is essential.

Starters

SMOKED SALMON CAKE WITH CHIVE CREAM CHEESE 40

SEARED COD WITH FENNEL FONDUE 43

BALLYSTRAW MUSSELS 44

MINI SHEPHERD'S PIES 47

POTATO AND CABBAGE SOUFFLÉ 48

IRISH GOAT'S CHEESE AND WILD MUSHROOM TERRINE 51

BANNOW BAY OYSTER SASHIMI-STYLE 52

WEXFORD STRAWBERRY SALAD WITH
A PEPPERED BLACKWATER CHEESE BASKET 55

Starters

WEXFORD MUSSELS

Irish children brought up near the coast gather mussels even though cultivated (much larger ones) are widely available. Like many other shellfish-loving adults, I enjoy a trip back to my childhood summer holidays, spent in Kilkea, County Clare. The satisfaction of gathering wild mussels, the exceptionally good flavour and texture, are what I like and this more than compensates for their small size. Wild mussels grow largest at the futhermost reach of the ebb tide. When gathering you must keep an eye on the incoming tide, particularly where there is a rip-tide, or you'll get more than wet feet!

Mussels are a bivalve with world-wide distribution. They grow in clusters attaching themselves to whatever presents itself with byssus-threads. They feed on nutrients filtered from sea water (often filtering 45 litres of water a day). Their dark-blue, blackish shells are familiar on rocky sea shores and in or near estuaries. Two similar species are found in Europe: the *Mytilis edulis* and *Mytilus galloprovincialis*; both akin to *Mytilis californianus*, found along the west coast of America.

An Irishman called Walton is credited with inventing the method of farming mussels. Shipwrecked in 1235 in the Bay of aiguillon on the western French coast he tried to make money by trapping seabirds in nets supported by poles. The poles were soon settled by clusters of baby mussels and he discovered a new way of making a living! The method is still used in parts of France. A commoner method now is to anchor rafts in suitable bays with suspended ropes on which the mussels grow and can be easily harvested.

Be cautious. Gather wild mussels from clean water and remember that in certain conditions mussels can harbour toxins. Typically, when a certain organism is present in the water, it is visible as a "red tide". Cultivated mussels are purified in tanks before being sold. Wild mussels are cleaned by placing them in salted water for two hours (more and they asphyxiate); a little oatmeal added to the water is said to plump them up. Use only fresh, live mussels; their shells should be closed or, when tapped, the mussels should pull their shells firmly closed. When cooked, after a few minutes, the shells should be open; throw away any that don't open.

FOOD TRENDS COME AND GO BUT THIS IS ONE RECIPE THAT HAS STOOD THE TEST OF TIME AT DUNBRODY, AND ONCE YOU'VE TAKEN YOUR FIRST BITE YOU'LL UNDERSTAND WHY. IT IS PERFECT FOR A DINNER PARTY AS IT CAN BE PREPARED SEVERAL HOURS IN ADVANCE, READY TO BE BROUGHT BACK TO ROOM TEMPERATURE AND DRESSED WITH A LITTLE SALAD.

SMOKED SALMON CAKE
with CHIVE CREAM CHEESE

225g/8oz smoked salmon slices

225g/8oz cream cheese

1 tbsp/1¼ US tablespoons snipped fresh chives

juice of ½ lemon

25g/1oz baby salad leaves

about 2 tbsp/2½ US tablespoons Dalkey mustard dressing (page 161)

FOR THE PANCAKES

50g/2oz / ½ cup plain flour

1 small egg

about 150ml/ ¼ pint/ ⅔ cup milk

sunflower oil, for frying

salt and freshly ground black pepper

lemon wedges, to serve

Serves 4

TO MAKE THE PANCAKES, sift the flour into a bowl with a pinch of salt, then make a well in the centre. Break the egg into the well and add a little of the milk. Mix the liquid ingredients together, then gradually beat in the flour until smooth. Beat in enough of the remaining milk until you have achieved the consistency of thin cream. Cover with cling film and leave to stand in the fridge for 20 minutes.

Heat a heavy-based frying pan. When hot, brush with the minimum of oil. Pour a small amount of the batter, about a quarter of the mix is right. Swirl it around until it is evenly and thinly spread over the bottom. Cook over a moderate to high heat for about 1 minute or until the edges are curling and the underside is golden. Flip over and cook the second side for 30 seconds or so until golden.

Turn the pancake onto a plate and repeat until you have four pancakes in total, lightly oiling the pan between pancakes. Leave to cool, then using a 5cm/ 2in cutter that is 5cm/2in deep, stamp out three circles from each pancake.

Using the same cutter, stamp out eight circles from the smoked salmon, then cut the remainder into strips and reserve. Whip the cream cheese in a bowl with the chives and lemon juice. Season to taste.

TO SERVE, line the cutter with cling film and set on a serving plate. Put a pancake round in the bottom of the cutter and add a spoonful of the chive cream cheese. Cover with a layer of the smoked salmon and then add another spoonful of the chive cream cheese. Repeat these layers and finish with a pancake round. Carefully remove the cutter and repeat until you have four in total. Place the salad leaves in a bowl, season and add enough of the dressing to lightly coat the leaves. Add a pile to each plate with the reserved smoked salmon strips. Drizzle around the remaining dressing and garnish with the lemon wedges.

SEARED COD WITH FENNEL FONDUE

JUDGING EXACTLY HOW LONG THE COD TAKES TO COOK CAN BE DIFFICULT, AS THE FILLETS VARY SO MUCH IN THICKNESS. A GOOD TIP IS TO KEEP AN EYE ON THE SIDE OF YOUR FISH FILLETS WHILE THEY ARE FRYING IN THE PAN. WHEN THEY LOOK HALF WAY COOKED, TURN THEM OVER AND FINISH COOKING THEM ON THE OTHER SIDE.

2 tbsp/2½ US tablespoons olive oil

1 shallot, finely chopped

1 small fennel bulb, finely chopped (with fennel sprigs reserved for garnish)

2 star anise

120ml/4fl oz/½ cup dry white wine

400ml/14fl oz/1¾ cups fennel-scented fish stock (page 167) or water

1 tbsp/1¼ US tablespoons crème fraîche

4 x 50g/2oz cod fillets, skin on and slashed half way through at 0.5 cm/¼ in intervals

coarse sea salt and freshly ground black pepper

herb oil, to garnish (page 158)

Serves 4

Heat half the olive oil in a pan and gently sauté the shallot, fennel and star anise for about 10 minutes until softened but not coloured. Pour in the white wine and allow to bubble right down for about 5 minutes until well reduced and syrupy.

Pour the fish stock or water into the pan and season to taste. Bring to the boil, then reduce the heat, cover with a lid and simmer gently for about 25 minutes until the fennel is completely tender and the mixture is fragrant.

Remove the star anise from the pan and stir in the crème fraîche. Simmer, uncovered for about 3 minutes. Ladle into a food processor or liquidiser and whizz until smooth. Pass the purée through a fine sieve set over a bowl, rubbing with the back of a ladle or wooden spoon. Cover the bowl with cling film and chill until needed.

Heat a heavy-based frying pan until searing hot and add the remaining olive oil. Add the cod fillets skin-side down and cook for about 2 minutes until the skin is crispy and lightly browned. Turn the fillets over and cook for another 2 minutes or so until just tender. Season lightly.

Meanwhile, pour the fennel fondue into a clean pan and reheat gently.

TO SERVE, ladle the fennel fondue into wide-rimmed serving bowls and arrange the cod fillets on top, skin side up. Drizzle around the herb oil and garnish with the reserved fennel fronds.

BALLYSTRAW MUSSELS

EVERYONE LOVES A BOWL OF STEAMING FRAGRANT MUSSELS. THEY SHOULD BE FAT, JUICY AND SMOTHERED IN HEAPS OF GARLIC AND HERB FLAVOURED CREAM. FOR A CHANGE I LIKE TO COOK THEM ON THE BARBECUE OVER SOME HICKORY WOOD CHIPS, WHICH IMPARTS A VERY SUBTLE FLAVOUR TO THE DISH.

2 tbsp/2 ½ US tablespoons olive oil

2 garlic cloves, thinly sliced

1 small onion, finely chopped

900g/2lb mussels, scrubbed clean

2 plum tomatoes, peeled, seeded and diced

120ml/4fl oz/½ cup white wine

120ml/4fl oz/½ cup cream

1 tbsp/1 ¼ US tablespoons torn fresh basil

1 tbsp/1 ¼ US tablespoons herb oil (page 158)

4 slices caramelised Dunbrody onion crostini (page 155)

salt and freshly ground black pepper

Serves 4

Heat the olive oil in a heavy-based pan. Add the garlic and sauté for 1 minute, then tip in the onion and continue to cook for another minute.

Add the mussels to the pan with the tomatoes and stir until well combined, then pour in the wine and allow to bubble up. Stir in the cream with the basil and herb oil, then cover and cook for 3-4 minutes, shaking the pan occasionally until all the mussels have opened; discard any that do not. Season to taste.

TO SERVE, ladle the mussels and liquor into wide-rimmed serving bowls and add a slice of the caramelised Dunbrody onion crostini to each one.

MINI SHEPHERD'S PIES

I COULD NEVER TIRE OF A PLATE OF SHEPHERD'S PIE. AND IN MY MIND IT IS ONE OF THE WORLD'S GREAT CLASSICS. THIS IS A VERSION THAT I HAVE DEVELOPED OVER THE YEARS BUT THE MAIN INGREDIENTS ARE STILL THE SAME. YOU COULD ALSO USE THE LEFTOVERS FROM THE SUNDAY ROAST LEG OF LAMB INSTEAD OF THE MINCE WITH EXCELLENT RESULTS.

1 shallot

1 tsp caster sugar

450g/1lb potatoes, well scrubbed

1 tbsp/1¼ US tablespoons olive oil

1 small onion, finely chopped

1 small leek, finely chopped

1 small carrot, finely chopped

1 garlic clove, crushed

225g/8oz lean minced lamb

1 tbsp/1¼ US tablespoons tomato purée

3 tbsp/3¾ US tablespoons milk

25g/1oz/¼ stick butter

2 tsp herb oil (page 158)

salt and freshly ground black pepper

fresh thyme leaves, to garnish

Serves 4

Preheat the oven to 180°C/350°F/Gas 4. Cut the shallot in half and then cut into thin slices lengthways, leaving the root intact. Arrange the slices on a non-stick baking sheet and sprinkle over the caster sugar. Bake for 5 minutes until lightly golden and caramelised. Remove from the heat and leave to cool completely.

Cover the potatoes with cold water in a pan and add a pinch of salt. Bring to the boil, then simmer for 15-20 minutes or until completely tender when pierced with the tip of a sharp knife. Drain in a colander and peel the potatoes while they are still hot.

Meanwhile, heat the olive oil in a pan. Add the onion, leek, carrot and garlic and sauté for 3-4 minutes until just beginning to soften but not colour. Stir the minced lamb into the pan and cook for 2-3 minutes until browned, breaking up any lumps with the back of a wooden spoon. Stir in the tomato purée and cook gently for another 10 minutes until completely tender. Season to taste and keep warm or reheat as needed.

Push the cooked peeled potatoes through a potato ricer or sieve, using a spatula. Quickly heat the milk in a pan. Beat the butter into the warm mashed potato and then add enough milk to make a smooth but firm purée. Season to taste.

TO SERVE, spoon the mince mixture into 6cm/2½in ring moulds set on warmed serving plates. Carefully remove the moulds. Using two dessert-spoons, shape the potato purée into quenelles and arrange four on top of each serving (or use a piping bag). Top with the caramelised shallot slices and drizzle around the herb oil. Garnish with the thyme leaves.

STARTERS

POTATO AND CABBAGE SOUFFLÉ

I HAVE MADE THIS RECIPE A THOUSAND TIMES AND IT ALWAYS WORKS, SO PLEASE DON'T BE AFRAID TO GIVE IT A GO. YOU CAN ACTUALLY PUT THESE SOUFFLÉS IN THE OVEN TWICE TO RISE A SECOND TIME JUST BEFORE SERVING. I NORMALLY USE LEFTOVER COOKED POTATOES OR MASH, BUT YOU CAN STEAM OR BOIL THEM WHOLE ESPECIALLY FOR THIS DISH. JUST LEAVE THEM TO COOL COMPLETELY BEFORE PEELING AND GRATING.

50g/2oz/½ stick butter

50g/2oz dried white breadcrumbs

50g/2oz ground walnuts

225g/8oz smoked cheese, grated (such as Gubbeen)

2 egg yolks

100g/4oz Savoy cabbage, thick stalks removed and finely shredded

100g/4oz cooked peeled potato, grated

5 egg whites

FOR THE BÉCHAMEL SAUCE

100g/4oz/1 stick butter

100g/4oz/1 cup plain flour

300ml/½ pint/1⅓ cups milk

salt and freshly ground black pepper

flowered watercress sprigs, to garnish (optional)

Serves 4

Preheat the oven to 180°C/350°F/Gas 4. Grease 4 x 200ml/7fl oz /1 scant cup capacity ramekins or heatproof cups with a little of the butter and freeze until firm. Repeat this three times in order to obtain a good coating. Mix together the breadcrumbs and walnuts and use to lightly coat the final layer of butter.

TO MAKE THE BÉCHAMEL SAUCE, melt the butter in a pan. Slowly add the flour and cook for 1 minute, stirring constantly until the mixture becomes a light coloured roux. Gradually pour in the milk, whisking constantly. Bring to the boil, again whisking constantly, then reduce the heat and simmer for 2-3 minutes until thickened and smooth. Stir the cheese into the sauce until melted, then remove from the heat and leave to cool a little. Season to taste and fold in the egg yolks.

Heat the remaining knob of butter in a frying pan. Add the cabbage and grated potato and cook over a low heat for about 5 minutes, tossing occasionally. Fold into the thick béchamel and then transfer to a large metal bowl.

Beat the egg whites in a separate bowl until soft peaks have formed, then carefully fold into the cabbage mixture. Divide among the prepared ramekins and gently tap each one on the work surface to expel any air bubbles. Arrange on a baking sheet and bake for 15-20 minutes or until well risen and lightly golden.

TO SERVE, set each soufflé on a warmed serving plate and garnish with the flowered watercress sprigs, if liked.

IRISH GOAT'S CHEESE AND WILD MUSHROOM TERRINE

THIS IS ONE OF MY FAVOURITE STARTERS. THE SAUTÉED MUSHROOMS COMPLEMENT THE SALTINESS OF THE GOAT'S CHEESE PERFECTLY. IT IS GOOD AS A CHEESE COURSE OR CUT INTO SMALL WEDGES AND SERVE AS PART OF AN ANTIPASTI PLATTER WITH CONNEMARA SMOKED LAMB OR PARMA HAM. OVEN DRIED TOMATOES (PAGE 159) AND SOME CROSTINI (PAGE 155). IT ALSO MAKES GREAT PICNIC FOOD WITH MY APRICOT CHUTNEY (PAGE 159) AS IT IS SO EASY TO TRANSPORT – THE POSSIBILITIES ARE ENDLESS.

1 tbsp/1¼ US tablespoons olive oil

3 shallots, finely chopped

1 garlic clove, crushed

175g/6oz forest mushrooms, chopped (such as chanterelle, oyster and shiitake)

225g/8oz soft goat's cheese, crumbled (from a log such as Mine Gabhar)

1 tbsp/1¼ US tablespoons wholegrain mustard

1 tbsp/1¼ US tablespoons chopped fresh flat-leaf parsley

1 poached pear, quartered and fanned out (page 122)

salt and freshly ground black pepper

fresh marjoram sprigs, to garnish (optional)

4 wafer-thin slices caramelised Dunbrody onion crostini (page155) (optional)

Serves 4–6

Heat the olive oil in a heavy-based frying pan. Add the shallots and garlic and sauté for about 2 minutes until softened but not coloured. Add the mushrooms, season generously and continue to sauté for 3-4 minutes until tender and all of the excess liquid has evaporated from the pan.

Remove the pan from the heat and add the goat's cheese with the mustard, parsley and a good grinding of pepper. Stir gently for a minute or two until some of the goat's cheese has just started to melt, tossing the pan occasionally. Be careful not to overcook this or you will end up with a processed cheese-type finish.

Transfer the goat's cheese mixture into a 600ml/1 pint loaf tin that is lined with cling film. Leave to cool completely, then cover with more cling film and chill for at least 2 hours, or overnight is best, to firm up.

TO SERVE, turn the terrine out on to a chopping board and peel away the cling film, then cut into individual slices. Arrange on serving plates with the fanned out poached pear. Garnish with the marjoram sprigs and serve with crostini, if liked.

BANNOW BAY OYSTERS SASHIMI-STYLE

ASK YOUR FISHMONGER TO OPEN THE OYSTERS FOR YOU. YOU'LL JUST NEED TO DOUBLE CHECK THAT THERE ARE NO BITS OF BROKEN SHELL INSIDE BEFORE USING THEM. ALTERNATIVELY YOU COULD ALWAYS TRY HAVING A GO YOURSELF. IT REALLY IS QUITE SIMPLE ONCE YOU GET THE HANG OF IT. AN OYSTER KNIFE REALLY IS A VERY GOOD INVESTMENT IF THIS IS SOMETHING THAT YOU ARE INTENDING TO DO REGULARLY.

12 oysters (native or Pacific)

1 tbsp/1¼ US tablespoons sesame seeds

about 225g/8oz coarse rock salt

6 tbsp/7½ US tablespoons dark soy sauce (such as Kikkoman)

finely grated rind and juice of 1 lime

1 tbsp/1¼ US tablespoons shredded root ginger

1 spring onion, finely shredded

4 tbsp/5 US tablespoons toasted sesame oil

2 garlic cloves, thinly sliced

Serves 4

Scrub the oyster shells then place one, wrapped in a clean tea towel on a firm surface with the flattest shell uppermost and the hinge pointing towards you. Gripping the oyster firmly, insert an oyster knife into the gap in the hinge and twist to snap the shells apart.

Slide the blade of the knife along the inside of the upper shell to sever the muscle that keeps the shells together. Lift the lid off the top shell, being careful not to spill any of the juices. Carefully clean away any bits of broken shell and finally run the knife under the oyster to loosen it from the shell. Repeat until all the oysters are opened, then arrange on a tray and place in the fridge until you are ready to serve.

Heat a frying pan over a medium to low heat and add the sesame seeds. Cook for 3-4 minutes, stirring regularly until they are lightly toasted. Tip out of the pan onto a plate and set aside until needed.

TO SERVE, arrange three oysters on a bed of rock salt on each serving plate. Mix together the soy sauce in a bowl with the lime rind and juice, then spoon over the oysters. Scatter the ginger, spring onion and reserved toasted sesame seeds on top. Leave to stand for 5 minutes to allow the flavours to develop. Meanwhile, heat the sesame oil in the frying pan and sauté until the garlic until golden and the sesame oil is nearly smoking. Drizzle over the oysters and serve immediately.

WEXFORD STRAWBERRY SALAD WITH A PEPPERED BLACKWATER CHEESE BASKET

THIS VERY SIMPLE STARTER IS A MASTERPIECE - EVERYONE WILL THINK YOU'VE BEEN SLAVING AWAY IN THE KITCHEN FOR HOURS. CHOOSE THE TYPE OF GOAT'S CHEESES YOU USE CAREFULLY, AS ITS FLAVOUR WILL DETERMINE THE SUCCESS OF THE DISH.

100g/4oz hard goat's cheese, grated (such as Blackwater)

about ½ tsp cracked black pepper

2 x 100g/4oz soft rinded goat's cheese, cut into chunks (such as Mine Gabhar)

100g/4oz small strawberries, hulled and halved

100g/4oz raspberries

good handful fresh mixed summer herbs (such as chives, dill, mint and oregano)

50g/2oz mixed baby salad leaves

2-3 tbsp/2½ -3¾ US tablespoons raspberry vinaigrette (page 161)

edible flowers, to garnish

Serves 4

Heat a non-stick frying pan until searing hot. Sprinkle a quarter of the grated hard goat's cheese into the centre of the pan in a circle that is about 10cm/4in in diameter. Add a good sprinkling of pepper and cook for 2-3 minutes until the fat starts to separate from the cheese and bubble. Remove from the heat and leave to cool for 1 minute.

Using a spatula, remove the melted cheese disc from the pan. Shape the cheese basket around the end of a straight-sided tall glass and hold for 30 seconds to 1 minute until set. Transfer to a wire rack and allow to cool completely. Repeat with the remaining ingredients until you have four cheese baskets in total.

Place the soft goat's cheese in a bowl with the strawberries, raspberries, herbs and mixed baby salad leaves. Drizzle over enough of the raspberry vinaigrette to barely coat the mixture.

TO SERVE, arrange the cheese baskets on serving plates and spoon in the dressed fruit and salad mixture, allowing it to tumble out on to the plates. Garnish with the edible flowers.

GOAT CHEESES

For over twenty years, in the townland of Ballynadrishoge, near the village of Blackwater in County Wexford, Anne and Luc Van Kampen have made their almost legendary cheese *Mine Gabhar*, an Irish farmhouse cheese made from goat's milk.

Even amongst the widespread community of highly individual and creative farmhouse cheesemakers scattered across every part of the island, the Van Kampens stand out as a couple who make exceptionally good cheeses. They have a houseful of international awards to prove it and my *Wexford strawberry salad with a peppered Blackwater cheese basket* (page 55) showcases them perfectly.

I take great pleasure in watching the skill they bring to their cheesemaking and the chance to just sit in the garden with old friends and enjoy tasting their cheeses over a glass of local apple juice.

Mine Gabhar is a small, delicate, finely handcrafted cheese. Its finely mottled, natural rind with its blue and white bloom is beautiful to behold. Inside is a pure white, thick, silky-smooth cheese which melts on the tongue. There is depth to the taste, a balanced combination of sweet, oakey, herbal flavours.

Ann and Luc also make an award-winning hard goat's cheese called *Blackwater*. Although similar in style to a mature gouda the use of goats rather than cows milk results in a cheese that is full of flavour and the drier texture makes it wonderful cheese for cooking.

They make a number of fresh French-style lactic curd cheeses in which they use only a small amount of rennet. They produce soft crottins and long log shapes that Luc sometimes sells fresh and sometimes allows to mature. *Croghan*, another important cheese in their range is an aromatic, semi-soft cheese, which has excellent melting qualities.

In Ireland each farmhouse cheese is made on only one farm, by one family, from the milk of cows, sheep, or goats. Goat's cheeses are made in many places in Ireland and, as with all farmhouse cheese, terroir, grass, natural herbage and the personality of the cheesemaker come together to make each cheese unique to its producer.

Light Bites

HADDOCK SMOKEY 64

PINT OF PRAWNS WITH A PRAWN AND GUINNESS CHASER 67

BEER BATTERED COCKTAIL SAUSAGES WITH MUSTARD MAYONNAISE 68

BOXTY POTATO CAKE SALAD 71

GOLDEN WONDER POTATO OMELETTE 72

KILMORE QUAY CRAB AND WATERCRESS SPRING ROLL 75

WILD MUSHROOM AND CASHEL BLUE TOASTIES 76

JAR OF COUNTRY PATÉ 79

Light Bites

DUNBRODY HENS

When I wake up in the morning and make a cup of tea, I go for a walk around the garden and stop to talk to my hens which are nourished by plentiful supplies of organic vegetables. They faithfully produce basketfuls of exceptionally tasty and well-flavoured, fresh eggs for the kitchen.

We found it hard to source a consistently reliable supplier and I thought it made sense to keep our own and have control over quality and year-round availability. Rhode Island Reds are a traditional Irish farmyard hen and hens are a part of the cycle of nature which is so beneficial to the kitchen garden. Hens need to be allowed to scratch about outdoors, as nature intended. They'll spend hours every day happily scrapping around, eating a variety of vegetables from the kitchen and garden, and seeking out all those interesting insects that abound in all this fresh green stuff. Add in a little protein and whole grains and you have happy hens who lay tasty eggs. The best accommodation for hens is a good solid wooden hen-house that's waterproof, draught-proof (but well ventilated) with perches and nest-boxes inside and access to their open air scratching area. Keeping hens is not rocket science, but if you're kind to them you'll be well rewarded.

HADDOCK SMOKEY

THIS IS COMFORT FOOD AT ITS BEST, FOREVER SATISFYING AND EASY TO PREPARE AHEAD. I LIKE TO USE UNDYED SMOKED HADDOCK AS IT HAS A MORE SUBTLE SUPERIOR FLAVOUR TO ITS BRIGHTLY COLOURED COUSIN. FOR A MORE DISTINCTIVE TASTE TRY USING KIPPERS. YOU'LL JUST NEED TO POACH THEM GENTLY FOR A COUPLE OF MINUTES BEFORE FLAKING THE FLESH, DISCARDING ANY SKIN AND BONE.

2 plum tomatoes, seeded and diced

450g/1lb smoked haddock fillet, skinned and cut into cubes (undyed if possible)

100g/4oz Cheddar cheese, grated

300ml/ ½ pint/1⅓ cups cream

freshly ground black pepper

white bread rolls and breadsticks with butter, to serve (page 155)

Serves 4

Preheat the oven to 180°C/350°F/Gas 4. Scatter half the tomatoes among four individual ovenproof dishes. Arrange the smoked haddock on top and sprinkle over half of the cheese. Scatter over the remaining tomatoes, season with pepper and pour over the cream. Arrange on a baking sheet and bake for 15-20 minutes until the smoked haddock is completely tender and the top is bubbling and golden brown.

TO SERVE, place the haddock smokey dishes directly on the table. Arrange the bread rolls and breadsticks in a separate basket and put on the table with a small pot of butter, then allow everyone to help themselves.

PINT OF PRAWNS WITH
A PRAWN AND GUINNESS CHASER

THIS DISH IS SIMPLICITY ITSELF. ALTHOUGH THE PRAWN INFUSION TAKES A BIT OF TIME IT CAN HAPPILY BE MADE IN ADVANCE AND FROZEN. BUY THE FRESHEST DUBLIN BAY PRAWNS (ALSO KNOWN AS LANGOUSTINES) YOU CAN FIND TO FILL THE PINT GLASSES BUT ORDINARY PRAWNS WILL BE FINE FOR THE CHASER. LUCKILY GOOD QUALITY SEAFOOD IS READILY AVAILABLE IN IRELAND, BUT IT IS ALWAYS WORTH BUYING FROM A RELIABLE SOURCE.

1kg/2 ¼ lb raw jumbo Dublin Bay prawns

1 tbsp/1 ¼ US tablespoons olive oil

450g/1lb raw prawns

1 onion, finely chopped

300g/11oz carrots, finely diced

50ml/2fl oz/ ¼ cup brandy

50g/2oz tomato purée

400ml/14fl oz/1 ¾ cups cream

2 tbsp/2 ½ US tablespoons Guinness

50g/2oz/ ½ stick butter, diced (at room temperature)

salt and freshly ground black pepper

Serves 4

Place the Dublin Bay prawns in a large pan and just cover with cold water. Bring to the boil, then remove from the heat and drain into a colander. The prawns should be cooked through but still very succulent and moist. Leave to cool.

Heat a large, heavy-based pan with the olive oil. Add the raw prawns, onion and carrots and sauté for 3-4 minutes. Pour in the brandy and allow to bubble down, then stir in the tomato purée. Pour in 1 litre/1 ³/₄ pints/ 4 ¹/₂ cups of water and bring to the boil, then reduce the heat and simmer for about 30 minutes until well flavoured and slightly reduced.

Remove the pan from the heat and strain the liquid through a fine sieve into a clean pan, then simmer until reduced by half. Pour in the cream and simmer for another 5 minutes until reduced by half again. Season to taste and keep warm or leave to cool and reheat as required – you should have about 400ml/14 fl oz/1 ³/₄ cups in total.

TO SERVE, place the prawn infusion in a small pan and add the Guinness, then allow to just warm through. Finally whisk in the butter. Arrange the cooked Dublin Bay prawns in old-fashioned pint glasses and place on serving plates. Pour the prawn and Guinness chaser into the shot glasses and set to one side.

BEER BATTERED COCKTAIL SAUSAGES WITH MUSTARD MAYONNAISE

A GREAT LITTLE APPETISER OR SNACK. I LOVE THE COMBINATION OF SUCCULENT SAUSAGE IN A CRISP BATTER DIPPED IN THE CREAMY MUSTARD FLAVOURED MAYONNAISE. THE SECRET IS OF COURSE, THE BATTER: MIXING IT QUICKLY AND USING IT IMMEDIATELY. FOR PRESENTATION PURPOSES I DRILLED HOLES INTO A CHEAP CHOPPING BOARD I PICKED UP, DEEP ENOUGH TO BE ABLE TO STICK DESSERT FORKS INTO. BUT THIS OF COURSE, IS AN OPTIONAL EXTRA!

sunflower oil, for deep-frying

450g/1lb cocktail sausages, skinned

FOR THE BEER BATTER

200g/7oz/1¾ cups plain flour, plus extra for dusting

50g/2oz/½ cup cornflour

120ml/4fl oz/½ cup lager

1 tbsp/1¼ US tablespoons wholegrain mustard

FOR THE MUSTARD MAYONNAISE

8 tbsp/10 US tablespoons mayonnaise

6 tbsp/7½ US tablespoons wholegrain mustard

juice of ½ lime

salt and freshly ground black pepper

Serves 4

Heat the oil in a deep-fat fryer to 180°C/350°F, until a small piece of white bread turns golden brown in about 30 seconds; or use a deep-sided pan and ensure that it is only half way full.

TO MAKE THE BEER BATTER, sift the flour and cornflour into a bowl. Make a well in the centre and add the lager and mustard. Whisk the liquid ingredients together and then gradually whisk into the flour mixture until you have achieved a smooth batter. Season to taste.

Dust the cocktail sausages in a light coating of flour and then dredge in the batter, shaking off any excess. Deep-fry for about 5 minutes or until cooked through and golden brown. You may have to do this in batches depending on the size of your fryer.

TO MAKE THE MUSTARD MAYONNAISE, place the mayonnaise in a bowl with the mustard and lime juice. Season to taste and mix until well combined.

TO SERVE, drain the beer battered cocktail sausages well on kitchen paper and stick on to forks or cocktail sticks. Arrange on serving plates with small bowls of the mustard mayonnaise on the side for dipping.

BOXTY POTATO CAKE SALAD

CRISPY ON THE OUTSIDE, SOFT AND BUTTERY INSIDE, THESE BOXTY POTATO CAKES WILL HELP YOU GET OVER THE WORST OF HANGOVERS. PANCETTA IS BASICALLY ITALIAN STREAKY BACON, BUT BECAUSE OF ITS FLAVOURFUL CURING IT IS OFTEN QUITE SUPERIOR – DRIER, PURER AND TASTIER. HOWEVER, IF YOU CAN'T GET HOLD OF IT, REPLACE WITH STREAKY BACON RASHERS.

450g/1lb potatoes, well scrubbed

50g/2oz rindless streaky bacon, finely chopped

2 spring onions, finely chopped

1 egg yolk

25g/1oz/¼ cup plain flour, plus extra for dusting

2 tbsp/2½ US tablespoons olive oil

knob of butter

4 slices pancetta (Italian crispy bacon)

25g/1oz baby salad leaves

about 1 tbsp/1¼ US tablespoons balsamic vinaigrette (page 161)

salt and freshly ground black pepper

fresh long chives, to garnish

Serves 4

Cover the potatoes with cold water in a pan and add a pinch of salt. Bring to the boil, then simmer for 15-20 minutes or until completely tender when pierced with the tip of a sharp knife. Drain in a colander and leave to cool completely.

When the potatoes have cooled, peel away the skins and then grate into a bowl – you should end up with about 350g/12oz in total. Heat a frying pan and add the bacon and sauté for 2-3 minutes until cooked through and lightly golden. Stir in the spring onions and continue to fry for another minute or so until softened. Tip into the grated potatoes with the egg yolk and sprinkle in the flour. Season generously and mix until just combined.

Divide the potato mixture into four and using a 10cm/4in cooking ring shape into patties, dusting with flour if neccessary. Arrange on a flat plate and cover loosely with cling film. Chill for at least 1 hour or up to 24 hours is fine to firm up.

Preheat the grill and heat the oil in a large heavy-based frying pan. Add the butter and once it has stopped foaming, add the boxty potato cakes. Cook for 2-3 minutes on each side until warmed through and golden brown.

Meanwhile, arrange the pancetta on a grill rack and cook for 2-3 minutes until crisp and golden, turning once. Drain well on kitchen paper.

TO SERVE, arrange the boxty potato cakes on warmed serving plates. Place the salad leaves in a bowl and quickly dress with the balsamic vinaigrette. Arrange a small pile on each potato cake and garnish with the pancetta and chives.

GOLDEN WONDER POTATO OMELETTE

THIS MAKES A FANTASTIC INEXPENSIVE SNACK OR, SERVED COLD, GREAT PICNIC FOOD. WE OFTEN CUT IT INTO SMALL CUBES AND SERVE THEM AS APPETISERS AT FUNCTIONS. I FIND IT KEEPS COVERED IN THE FRIDGE FOR UP TO TWO DAYS. I LIKE TO USE A NON-STICK FRYING PAN BUT A WELL-SEASONED HEAVY-BASED FRYING PAN ALSO WORKS WELL, IT'S JUST MORE DIFFICULT TO TURN THE OMELETTE OVER.

3 tbsp/3¾ US tablespoons olive oil

1 onion, thinly sliced

900g/2lb small potatoes, peeled (a waxy variety such as Nicola is best)

6 eggs

salt and freshly ground black pepper

lightly dressed mixed salad and oven dried tomatoes, to serve (page 159)

Serves 4

Heat 2 tbsp/2^1/$_2$ US tablespoons of the oil in a non-stick frying pan that is about 23-25cm/9-10in in diameter. Add the onion and sauté for 2-3 minutes until softened but not coloured. Using a mandolin or food processor, thinly slice the potatoes. Dry well in a clean tea towel and add to the pan, tossing to combine. Season generously, reduce the heat and cover with a lid or plate, then cook gently for 20-25 minutes until cooked through and lightly golden. Turn them over once or twice and shake the pan occasionally to ensure that they cook evenly.

Break the eggs into a large bowl, add a good pinch of seasoning, then whisk lightly with a fork. When the onion and potato mixture is cooked, drain off any excess oil and quickly stir into the beaten eggs.

Wipe out the frying pan and use to heat the remaining olive oil. Tip in the potato and egg mixture, stirring for the first 2 minutes and then press it down gently. Cook for another 3 minutes until there is virtually no raw egg mixture left on top of the omelette, pushing down the sides with a spatula for a curved edge. Invert onto a flat plate and slide the omelette back into the pan. Cook for another 5 minutes until just cooked through but still very moist in the centre.

TO SERVE warm or cold, turn the omelette on to a chopping board and cut into wedges. Place a wedge on each serving plate and serve with separate bowls of mixed salad and oven dried tomatoes to hand around.

KILMORE QUAY CRAB AND WATERCRESS SPRING ROLL

FROZEN SPRING ROLL WRAPPERS ARE READILY AVAILABLE FROM ORIENTAL SUPERMARKETS AND JUST NEED TO BE THAWED OUT BEFORE USING. FOR A SLIGHTLY DIFFERENT BUT EQUALLY GOOD RESULT, USE TWO LAYERS OF FILO PASTRY CUT INTO 25CM/10IN SQUARES FOR EACH SPRING ROLL.

1 tbsp/1¼ US tablespoons mayonnaise

1 tsp Dijon mustard

225g/8oz fresh white crabmeat

1 tbsp/1¼ US tablespoons chopped fresh mixed herbs (such as basil and coriander)

50g/2oz watercress, well picked over, plus extra to garnish

4 x 25cm/10in spring roll wrappers, thawed

1 egg yolk mixed with 2 tsp water

sunflower oil, for deep-frying

about 4 tbsp/5 US tablespoons chilli jam (page 160)

salt and freshly ground black pepper

Serves 4

Place the mayonnaise in a small bowl and beat in the mustard. Finely flake the crabmeat with a fork, removing any stray pieces of shell or cartilage as you go. Place in a bowl and add the mustard mayonnaise, the mixed herbs and watercress. Stir well to combine and season to taste.

Place a spring roll wrapper at an angle on a chopping board so that one of the corners points towards you. Brush around the edges with egg wash and then spoon about a quarter of the crab filling in a line near the top corner. Fold over to enclose and then roll it towards you a little. Fold in the sides and continue to roll up into a nice cylinder shape. Place on a non-stick baking sheet and repeat with the remaining ingredients until you have four spring rolls in total. Lightly brush with the remaining egg wash and chill for 30 minutes.

When ready to serve, pour enough of the oil into a deep-fat fryer or deep-sided pan to a depth of 6-7.5cm/2½-3in and heat to 180°C/350°F, or until a small piece of white bread turns golden brown in about 30 seconds. Deep-fry the spring rolls for 3-4 minutes or until crisp on all sides and lightly golden. Drain well on kitchen paper.

TO SERVE, using a sharp knife, cut off very ends of each spring roll so that they will sit well on the plate, then cut each one in half on the diagonal. Set on serving plates and drizzle over the chilli jam. Garnish with the watercress.

WILD MUSHROOM AND CASHEL BLUE TOASTIES

CASHEL BLUE IS A SEMI-SOFT FARMHOUSE BLUE CHEESE MADE FROM UNPASTEURISED COWS MILK IN COUNTY TIPPERARY. IT IS NOW ONE OF THE MOST WIDELY AVAILABLE IRISH CHEESES, WITH EXCELLENT DISTRIBUTION IN UK SUPERMARKETS AND SPECIALIST STORES. HOWEVER, THESE TOASTIES WOULD ALSO BE GOOD MADE WITH ANY SOFT BLUE CHEESE, SUCH AS GORGONZOLA OR DOLCELATTE. JUST BE CAREFUL NOT TO OVERCOOK THE CHEESE OR IT WILL BECOME STRINGY AND RUBBERY.

2 tbsp/2½ US tablespoons olive oil, plus extra for drizzling

2 shallots, finely chopped

350g/12oz forest mushrooms, sliced (such as chanterelle, oyster and shiitake)

120ml/4fl oz/½ cup white wine

120ml/4fl oz/½ cup cream

2 tbsp/2½ US tablespoons chopped fresh mixed herbs (such as flat-leaf parsley, basil and chives)

1 French baguette, cut into 12 slices on the diagonal (ends discarded)

25g/1oz/¼ stick butter, diced (at room temperature)

100g/4oz Cashel blue cheese, crumbled

salt and freshly ground black pepper

chopped fresh parsley, to garnish

Serves 4

Preheat a heavy-based griddle pan. Heat the olive oil in a frying pan. Add the shallots and sauté for 2 minutes until softened but not coloured. Tip in the mushrooms, season generously and continue to sauté for another 2-3 minutes until tender.

Pour the wine into the pan and allow to bubble down and reduce by half. Stir in the cream and herbs and allow to cook for a few minutes until slightly reduced and thickened.

Meanwhile, add the slices of bread to the heated griddle pan and toast until marked on both sides. Remove from the heat and drizzle a little olive oil over each one.

Remove the mushroom and cream mixture from the heat and whisk in the butter, then fold in the Cashel blue cheese until just beginning to melt.

TO SERVE, arrange the toasts on warmed serving plates and spoon the wild mushroom and Cashel blue cream on top. Garnish with the parsley.

JAR OF COUNTRY PATÉ

I JUST LOVE THIS WONDERFULLY TENDER AND DELICATELY FLAVOURED PATÉ. IRISH LAMBS LIVER IS AVAILABLE FROM EARLY SPRING THROUGH TO THE END OF THE SUMMER AND IS JUST PERFECT FOR THIS DISH. IT IS ALSO VERY CHEAP – BUY THE FRESHEST YOU CAN FIND. A LITTLE OF THIS GOES A LONG WAY, ESPECIALLY WHEN YOU SERVE IT WITH SOME CRISP TOASTS AND A DOLLOP OF MY APRICOT CHUTNEY.

400g/14oz lambs liver, thinly sliced and cut into strips

1 small onion, finely chopped

2 tbsp/2½ US tablespoons snipped fresh chives

50g/2oz/scant ½ cup plain flour

2 tbsp/2½ US tablespoons olive oil

350g/12oz/3½ sticks butter (at room temperature)

6 tbsp/7½ US tablespoons brandy, plus a little extra if necessary

100g/4oz/1 stick clarified butter (page 160)

about 8 tbsp/10 US tablespoons apricot chutney (page 159)

8-12 slices Dunbrody caramelised onion crostini (page 155)

salt and freshly ground black pepper

Serves 4-6

Heat a large frying pan until searing hot. Place the lambs liver in a bowl with the onion and chives. Sprinkle over the flour and season, then mix until well combined. Add the olive oil and a knob of the butter to the pan and then tip in the lambs liver mixture. Sauté for 4-5 minutes until the lambs liver is well sealed and lightly browned all over.

Pour the brandy over the lambs liver mixture and set alight, then use to deglaze the bottom of the pan by scraping off any sediment with a wooden spoon. Transfer to a food processor and add the remaining butter, then blitz until smooth. Season to taste and add another dash of brandy if you think it needs it.

Pour the country paté into a 900ml/1½ pint Kilner jar, tapping it gently on the work surface to ensure that it settles evenly and to remove any tiny air bubbles. Leave to cool completely and then pour over the clarified butter to seal completely. Close the jar and chill for at least 4 hours or overnight is best to firm up.

TO SERVE, spoon the country paté on to serving plates and add a dollop of the apricot chutney and a couple of slices of the crostini.

KILMORE QUAY

Kilmore Quay is a working fishing port with picturesque thatched cottages and is popular with visitors in search of sea angling. With good fishing grounds off South Wexford the boats land a wide variety of fresh fish and shellfish but many of the fishermen specialise in scallops, lobsters and crabs. Kilmore Quay crab is highly regarded and more abundant than lobster; there is a crab processing plant in the village. I use a great deal of it in the kitchen, for dishes such as my *Kilmore Quay crab and watercress spring roll* (Page 52). Much of the catch is snapped up by wholesalers on the quayside, but some goes to the central fish markets before being exported to mainland Europe.

Crab is one of my favourite foods "straight to the plate". I once lived in a thatched cottage in the village and know that being on the quay when the crab and lobster boats unload gets you first pick - and the fun of striking a bargain. As the most favoured part of the crab, the white meat comes from the claws only, choosing your own gives you the advantage that you can pick the males which have larger claws. Unless you buy them cooked, it's important that crabs are freshly caught and still alive when you buy them. Be careful how you pick them up - there's a knack of handling live crabs and lobsters to avoid being painfully nipped.

Although the are many types of crab, the main culinary variety in Ireland is the common or European crab, with a maximum width of about 25cm/10in they can weigh up to 5kg/11lb. The hard shell is pink or reddish brown with black tips to the claws. Worldwide there are 4,500 species of crab, from the oyster crab the size of a pea to the giant Japanese spider crab. North American varieties are not the same as those in Europe. On the Pacific coast (from Alaska to Mexico), the Dunganess crab is a different colour, and the claws are smaller to European crabs, but it is similar. As is the east Atlantic coast variety which is simply called the edible crab.

Mains

ROAST RACK OF LAMB IN IRISH STEW CONSOMMÉ 88

SEARED FILLET OF BEEF WITH CRISPY ONIONS AND
HORSERADISH CREAM 91

LOIN OF BACON WITH AN IRISH MIST GLAZE 92

OVEN BAKED POUSSIN WITH SAGE AND ROASTED GARLIC 95

CIDER GLAZED FILLET OF SALMON 96

TURBOT WITH CRISPY POTATO SCALES 99

HOOK HEAD FISHERMAN'S PIE 100

RACK OF DUBLIN BAY PRAWNS WITH MEAD SALSA 103

DOYLE'S DUBLIN CODDLE 104

Mains

ATLANTIC SALMON

The rivers Suir, Nore and Barrow come together below the town of New Ross, then flow down past Waterford city and port, down the tidal estuary, past the bottom of the garden of Dunbrody House, past Hook Head and its ancient lighthouse, into the Atlantic Ocean. All along the way there is good game fishing, with excellent fly fishing up river towards Inistioge. Fly fishing with a rod for salmon by no means guarantees a fish and can try the patience and, to a degree, test the luck of a fisherman.

There is a lot of skill involved in playing a strong and wily salmon before reeling him in and landing him. For me, a day on the river in the company of friends is a rare enough pleasure but work and play occasionally combine with the hope of a wild Irish salmon for the pot as a reward, and the look of triumphant pleasure says it all! When a day's fishing ends well, buying a pint of stout in the village pub is the traditional way of celebrating with your friends. If they are really lucky I might take them home and make my *Cider glazed fillet of salmon* (page 96).

Atlantic salmon is a migratory fish; its territory extends from Portugal to Norway, across to Greenland and on to North America. It has a fatty, deep-pink flesh with a superb rich flavour. It's a seasonal treat and fished for in Ireland from January to early September, depending upon the river.

ROAST RACK OF LAMB IN IRISH STEW CONSOMMÉ

I NEVER TIRE OF A BOWL OF STEAMING HOT STEW. THIS IS A VERSION
I HAVE DEVELOPED OVER THE YEARS, BUT THE MAIN INGREDIENTS ARE
STILL THE SAME AS MY MOTHER USES, AND HER MOTHER BEFORE HER.

1kg/2¼ lb scrag end of neck of lamb

2 leeks

2 carrots, roughly chopped

1 large onion, finely diced

2 celery sticks, roughly chopped

1 large bay leaf

1 large fresh thyme sprig

small handful flat-leaf parsley stalks

few black peppercorns

*2 x 6-bone best end of lamb, each about
275-350g/10-12oz*

175g/6oz small carrots

275g/10oz baby new potatoes

1 tbsp/1¼ US tablespoons olive oil

salt and freshly ground black pepper

*fresh rosemary and thyme sprigs,
to garnish*

Serves 4

Place the neck of lamb in a large stockpot. Roughly chop one of the leeks and add with the roughly chopped carrots, half of the onion, the celery, herbs and peppercorns. Cover with at least 1.75 litres/3 pints/8 cups of cold water. Bring to the boil, season lightly and then simmer gently, uncovered, for about 2 hours until reduced by nearly two-thirds — you'll need 450ml/³⁄₄ pint/2 cups of lovely, sweet stock in total. Skim off any scum or grease that rises to the surface with a large spoon. Strain the stock through a fine sieve into a large jug and ideally leave to cool overnight so that you can scrape off any fat that has settled on top.

Preheat the oven to 200°C/400°F/Gas 6. Season the racks of lamb and place in a small roasting tin. Roast for 20-25 minutes, or a little longer, depending on how pink you like your lamb. Remove from the oven and set aside in a warm place to rest for 10-15 minutes.

Meanwhile, peel and shape the small carrots and baby potatoes into neat barrels. Add to the lamb stock with the remaining onion and bring to a simmer. Cook gently for 10-15 minutes until the carrots and potatoes are completely tender but are still holding their shape. Season to taste.

Meanwhile, heat the olive oil in a frying pan. Cut the remaining leek into julienne (long thin strips) and add to the pan, then sauté for 3-4 minutes until softened but not coloured. Season to taste.

TO SERVE, carve the rested racks of lamb into chops. Place the leek julienne in the centre of each warmed wide-rimmed serving bowl and spoon around the Irish stew consommé. Arrange the lamb chops on top of the leeks and garnish with the rosemary and thyme sprigs.

SEARED FILLET OF BEEF WITH CRISPY ONIONS AND HORSERADISH CREAM

THIS WOULD MAKE A WONDERFUL LIGHT LUNCH OR SUPPER, AS IT IS FULL OF COMPLEMENTARY FLAVOURS AND TEXTURES - AND CAN EASILY BE SCALED UP TO MAKE A MORE SUBSTANTIAL DISH FOR SUNDAY LUNCH OR DINNER. THE MEAT IS THE HERO HERE, SO TRY TO USE GRASS-FED OR ORGANIC BEEF THAT HAS BEEN PROPERLY HUNG.

450g/1lb fillet of beef (well hung)

1 tbsp/1¼ US tablespoons olive oil

50g/2oz mixed salad leaves with herbs

1-2 tbsp/1¼ -2½ US tablespoons balsamic vinaigrette (page 161)

4 oven dried tomatoes (page 159)

FOR THE HORSERADISH CREAM

2 tbsp/2½ US tablespoons mayonnaise

1 tbsp/1¼ US tablespoons creamed horseradish

squeeze lemon juice

FOR THE CRISY ONIONS

sunflower oil, for deep-frying

50g/2oz/½ cup plain flour

1 large onion, thinly sliced

salt and freshly ground black pepper

Serves 4

Heat an ovenproof griddle pan until very hot. Season the beef fillet. Add the olive oil to the pan and then add the beef and brown well for 10 minutes on all sides until you have achieved a nice, thick crust. Remove from the heat and leave to stand in a warm place until the beef has relaxed. This will take at least 10 minutes, but you could leave the beef to stand for up to 2 hours, provided it is not in too hot a place.

TO MAKE THE HORSERADISH CREAM, place the mayonnaise in a small bowl with the creamed horseradish and lemon juice. Season to taste and mix until well combined. Cover with cling film and chill until needed.

TO MAKE THE CRISPY ONION RINGS, heat the oil in a deep-fat fryer to 180°C/350°F, until a small piece of white bread turns golden brown in about 30 seconds; or use a deep-sided pan and ensure that it is only half-way full.

Place the flour on a plate and season generously, then use to lightly dust the onion slices, shaking off any excess. Deep-fry for 4-5 minutes or until golden brown. Spread out on to kitchen paper and allow to cool and crisp up by lifting them occasionally to separate.

TO SERVE, when the beef has rested, transfer it to a carving board. Use a very sharp carving knife to cut it into slices. Place the mixed salad leaves with herbs in a bowl and add enough of the vinaigrette to lightly coat the leaves. Arrange the beef on serving plates with a dollop of the horseradish cream, the dressed salad, a small pile of the crispy onion rings and an oven dried tomato.

THE LOIN OF BACON IS MOST OFTEN USED FOR BACK RASHERS BUT IT ALSO MAKES A WONDERFUL JOINT OR CAN BE CUT INTO BACON CHOPS. MOST BACON NOW DOESN'T NEED TO BE SOAKED OVERNIGHT, BUT IT IS PROBABLY WORTH CHECKING WITH YOUR BUTCHER.

LOIN OF BACON WITH AN IRISH MIST GLAZE

900g/2lb loin of bacon (Canadian back bacon)

2 tbsp/2½ US tablespoons Irish Mist

4 tbsp/5 US tablespoons honey

100ml/3½ fl oz/7 US tablespoons cider

12 whole cloves

25g/1oz/¼ stick butter

2 tbsp/2½ US tablespoons olive oil

8 small Savoy cabbage leaves, trimmed down into cups

FOR THE POTATO CAKES

450g/1lb potatoes, well scrubbed

1 egg yolk

25g/1oz/¼ cup plain flour, plus extra for dusting

salt and freshly ground black pepper

Serves 4

Place the loin of bacon in a large pan and cover with cold water. Bring to the boil, then reduce the heat and simmer for 1 hour until completely tender.

TO MAKE THE POTATO CAKES, cover the potatoes with cold water in a pan and add a pinch of salt. Bring to the boil, then simmer for 15-20 minutes or until completely tender. Drain in a colander and leave to cool completely.

When the potatoes have cooled, peel away the skins and then grate into a bowl. Add the egg yolk and sprinkle in the flour. Season generously and mix until just combined. Divide the mixture into four and using a 10cm/4in cooking ring, shape into patties, using a little extra flour for dusting if neccessary. Arrange on a flat plate and cover loosely with cling film. Chill for at least 1 hour or up to 24 hours is fine to firm up.

Preheat the oven to 180°C/350°F/Gas 4. Place the Irish Mist in a pan with the honey and cider, then heat gently until dissolved. Remove the loin of bacon from the water and leave until cool enough to handle, then trim away the rind and excess fat. Slash the remaining thin layer of fat in a criss-cross pattern and stud with cloves.

Place the clove-studded loin of bacon in a small roasting tin and brush all over with the Irish Mist glaze, pouring any remainder around the joint. Bake for 15-20 minutes until completely heated through and well glazed, basting occasionally.

Remove the bacon from the oven and leave in a warm place for at least 10 minutes. Heat the oil in a heavy-based frying pan. Add a knob of the butter and once foaming, add the potato cakes. Cook for 2-3 minutes on each side until warmed through and golden brown. Blanch the cabbage cups in a pan of boiling salted water until just tender but still holding their shape. Drain well and toss in the remaining knob of butter. Season to taste.

TO SERVE, carve the bacon into slices. Place a potato cake on each warmed serving plate and arrange the slices of bacon on top. Add the Savoy cabbage cups and then drizzle around the remaining glaze left in the tin.

OVEN BAKED POUSSIN WITH SAGE AND ROASTED GARLIC

POUSSINS ARE THE SMALLEST CHICKENS AVAILABLE TO BUY. I LIKE THEM BECAUSE THEY ARE VERY TENDER AND QUICK TO COOK. EACH ONE IS A PERFECT PORTION SIZE, MAKING THEM GREAT FOR DINNER PARTIES.

12 spring onions, trimmed

2 tbsp/2 ½ US tablespoons olive oil

4 oven-ready poussins

75g/3oz/³/₄ stick butter (at room temperature)

8 fresh sage leaves, plus extra to garnish

2 garlic cloves, thinly sliced

225g/8oz Swiss chard, thick stalks removed and roughly chopped

coarse sea salt and freshly ground black pepper

Serves 4

Preheat the oven to 180°C/350°F/Gas 4. Arrange the spring onions in a roasting tin. Season generously and toss in half the olive oil until evenly coated.

Loosen the skin around the neck of each poussin and push under a little of the butter until evenly spread over the breast, then push a sage leaf down each side so that they are clearly visible.

Arrange the poussins on the bed of spring onions and scatter over the garlic. Drizzle over the remaining olive oil and season to taste. Roast for 35 minutes until the poussins are completely tender and golden brown. Leave to rest in a warm place for at least 10 minutes.

TO SERVE, heat the remaining knob of butter in a pan and quickly sauté the chard for a minute or two until wilted. Season to taste and divide among warmed serving plates. Add some of the roasted spring onions to each one and sit a poussin on top. Scatter over the sage leaves to garnish.

MAINS

CIDER GLAZED FILLET OF SALMON

THE BEST WAY TO TREAT FISH IS SIMPLY. THE FRESHEST SALMON IS COVERED WITH A HOT MARINADE THAT COOKS AND SEALS THE OUTSIDE ON IMPACT. THEN IT IS COOKED TO CREATE A CRISP EXTERIOR, WHILE THE INSIDE OF THE FISH REMAINS MOIST. THIS RECIPE IS PERFECT FOR LAZY SUMMER DAYS AND COULD BE COOKED WITH VERY LITTLE EFFORT ON THE BARBECUE. CIDER IS A VERSITLE INGREDIENT IN COOKING AND IS MADE IN CLONMEL, WHICH IS QUITE NEAR DUNBRODY.

120ml/4fl oz/ ½ cup dry cider

1 tbsp/1¼ US tablespoons honey

4 x 175g/6oz salmon fillets, scaled and boned

2 lemons, halved and pips removed

knob of butter

350g/12oz tender young spinach leaves

1 tbsp/1¼ US tablespoons white wine

coarse sea salt and freshly ground black pepper

Serves 4

Preheat the oven to 180°C/350°F/Gas 4. Place the cider in a small pan with the honey and season with pepper. Bring to the boil and then reduce by half until slightly sticky and syrupy.

Arrange the salmon fillets in a non-stick metallic dish, skin-side up. Pour over the hot cider mixture and then set aside for 10 minutes to allow the flavours to develop.

Heat a large heatproof frying pan. Season the flesh side of the salmon fillets and add to the pan flesh side down. Cook for 2 minutes, brushing the top with some of the remaining cider glaze so that the fish fillets begin to caramelise.

Turn the salmon fillets over and brush with the remaining cider glaze. Add the lemon halves to the pan, cut side down and then transfer to the oven. Bake for 6-8 minutes until the salmon is tender and lightly caramelised.

Meanwhile, heat the butter in a pan. Add the spinach and season to taste. Sauté for 1 minute until just beginning to wilt, then drizzle over the wine and continue to cook until tender.

TO SERVE, drain any excess liquid from the spinach and divide among warmed serving plates. Arrange a salmon fillet on each one to serve with a caramelised lemon half on the side to garnish.

TURBOT WITH CRISPY POTATO SCALES

CARRAGEEN MOSS IS A SEAWEED FOUND ON THE SEASHORES OF
IRELAND. HOWEVER ANY EDIBLE SEAWEED WOULD WORK IN THIS
RECIPE, JUST BE CAREFUL NOT TO HEAT IT TOO LONG IN THE CREAM
AS THE NATURAL GELATINE WILL CURDLE THE SAUCE.

*4 waxy baby potatoes, peeled
(such as Nicola)*

*50g/2oz/½ stick clarified butter
(page 160)*

1 tbsp/1¼ US tablespoons olive oil

*4 x 150g/5oz turbot fillets,
skinned and boned*

2 large leeks, thinly sliced

2 tbsp/2½ US tablespoons white wine

200ml/7fl oz/⅘ cup cream

*40g/1½ oz cleaned, well dried carrageen
moss, finely chopped (seaweed)*

salt and freshly ground black pepper

Serves 4

Preheat the grill to medium. Using a mandolin or food processor, cut the potatoes into thin slices. Heat half of the clarified butter with the oil in a frying pan until hot but not smoking. Add the potatoes and blanch for 2 minutes until softened but not coloured.

Season the turbot fillets and arrange the potato slices in an overlapping layer like fish scales on top of each one. Return the frying pan to the heat and tip away any excess fat. Add the turbot fillets, potato slices up and seal the bottom of the fillets for 1 minute.

Meanwhile, heat a knob of the remaining clarified butter in a pan. Add the leeks and sauté for about 5 minutes until softened but not coloured.

Carefully transfer the turbot fillets to a grill rack and place under the grill for 5 minutes until cooked through and the potato slices are golden brown.

Heat the rest of the clarified butter in a pan and pour in the wine. then cook for another 2 minutes. Season to taste and add the cream and carrageen moss. Heat gently until warmed through. Season with pepper.

TO SERVE, spoon the leeks on to warmed serving plates and arrange a piece of turbot on top of each one. Drizzle the seaweed butter sauce around the edges of the plate.

HOOK HEAD FISHERMAN'S PIE

1 egg

40g/1½ oz/3 US tablespoons butter

50g/2oz cornflakes, lightly crushed

25g/1oz fresh white breadcrumbs

2 tbsp/2½ US tablespoons chopped
fresh mixed herbs (such as basil and
flat-leaf parsley)

50g/2oz smoked salmon, cut into small pieces

6 spring onions, finely chopped

120ml/4fl oz/½ cup white wine

450ml/¾ pint/2 cups fennel
scented fish stock (page 167)

225g/8oz firm fish fillets, skinned, boned
and cut into bite-sized chunks (such as
cod, haddock, salmon and sea bass)

75g/3oz raw peeled Dublin Bay
prawns (or tiger prawns)

75g/3oz mussels, scrubbed

175ml/6fl oz/¾ cup cream

1 tbsp/1¼ US tablespoons chopped
fresh flat-leaf parsley

salt and freshly ground black pepper

lightly dressed green salad, to serve

Serves 4

WHENEVER I PUT THESE PIES ON THE MENU THEY WALK OUT OF THE DOOR. I NORMALLY USE A MIXTURE OF FISH, BUT YOU COULD USE JUST ONE VARIETY. SERVE IT WITH A FRESH GREEN SALAD SCATTERED WITH A HANDFUL OF EDIBLE FLOWER FOR SIMPLICITY.

Place the egg in a small pan and just cover with water, then cook for 10 minutes until hard-boiled. Drain and rinse under cold running water, then remove the shell and finely chop. Melt 15g/½oz/1 US tablespoon of the butter in a pan and remove from the heat. Stir in the chopped hard-boiled egg with the cornflakes, breadcrumbs and mixed herbs. Season to taste and set aside until needed.

Preheat the grill to medium. Melt the remaining 25g/1oz/2 US tablespoons of the butter in a pan and add the smoked salmon and spring onions. Sauté for 2-3 minutes without colouring. Pour in the wine and reduce by half, then add the stock and bring to a simmer.

Tip the fish and shellfish into the simmering stock and then stir in the cream and parsley. Cover and simmer gently for 2-3 minutes until the fish is cooked through and all of the mussels have opened; discard any that do not. Season to taste

Transfer into four individual ovenproof dishes and scatter the reserved breadcrumb mixture on top. Place under the grill for 5 minutes or until bubbling and lightly golden.

TO SERVE, bring the individual fish pies straight to the table with a separate bowl of salad and allow everyone to help themselves.

RACK OF DUBLIN BAY PRAWNS WITH MEAD SALSA

28 raw jumbo Dublin Bay prawns

olive oil, for brushing

knob of butter

1 tbsp/1¼ US tablespoons white wine

350g/12oz ruby chard or spinach, thick stems removed

FOR THE MEAD SALSA

½ small red, yellow and green pepper, seeded and finely diced

1 small mild red chilli, seeded and finely chopped

1 plum tomato, seeded and diced

1 small red onion, finely chopped

5 fresh mint leaves, shredded

2 tbsp/2½ US tablespoons mead or champagne

juice of 1 lime

3 tbsp/3¾ US tablespoons olive oil

salt and freshly ground black pepper

Serves 4

THIS IS A WONDERFUL SUMMER DISH WITH A LOVELY COMBINATION OF FLAVOURS. IT NOT ONLY LOOKS AND TASTES FANTASTIC BUT IS ALSO DECEPTIVELY EASY TO MAKE. TRY USING RAW PEELED TIGER PRAWNS AS A GOOD ALTERNATIVE. MEAD IS A FERMENTED HONEY-BASED DRINK MADE SINCE CELTIC TIMES, WITH A LIMITED AVAILABILITY BUT CHAMPAGNE IS A GOOD ALTERNATIVE.

TO MAKE THE MEAD SALSA, place the red, yellow and green pepper in a bowl with the chilli, tomato, red onion, mint, mead or champagne, lime juice and olive oil.

Break the heads off the Dublin Bay prawns and then carefully remove the shells, leaving the tails intact. Heat a large griddle pan until searing hot. Run 2 x 20cm/8in bamboo skewers through seven of the peeled prawns and repeat until you have four racks in total. Season to taste.

Brush the griddle pan with a little oil and add the racks of prawns, presentation side down. Cook for 1-2 minutes on each side until cooked through and lightly seared.

Meanwhile, heat the butter and wine in a pan. Tip in the ruby chard or spinach and season generously, then sauté for a minute or two until just wilted. Remove from the heat and drain away any excess liquid.

TO SERVE, divide the sautéed ruby chard among warmed serving plates and place a rack of the prawns on top of each one. Drizzle over the mead salsa and serve the remainder in a small bowl at the table.

DOYLE'S DUBLIN CODDLE

THIS IS MY TWIST ON A DISH THAT HAS BEEN AROUND SINCE THE EIGHTEENTH CENTURY. TRADITIONALLY IT WAS MADE ON PAY DAY OR ON A SATURDAY NIGHT AND LEFT SIMMERING ON THE STOVE, AS IT WAS NOT KNOWN WHAT TIME THE MAN OF THE HOUSE WOULD RETURN HOME FROM THE PUB.

225g/8oz rindless streaky bacon, cut into lardons

1 potato, diced

1 leek, thinly sliced

1 large carrot, diced

1 tsp fresh thyme leaves, plus extra to garnish

400ml/14fl oz/1¾ cups kitchen garden vegetable stock (page 168)

4 large butcher-style pork sausages

FOR THE POTATO PURÉE

450g/1lb potatoes, well scrubbed

3 tbsp/3¾ US tablespoons milk

25g/1oz/¼ stick butter

salt and freshly ground black pepper

Serves 4

TO MAKE THE POTATO PURÉE, Cover the potatoes with cold water in a pan and add a pinch of salt. Bring to the boil, then simmer for 15-20 minutes or until completely tender when pierced with the tip of a sharp knife.

Heat a pan and sauté the bacon in the pan for 2-3 minutes until it has begun to release its fat. Add the potato, leek, carrot and thyme and continue to cook for 4-5 minutes until softened but not coloured.

Pour the vegetable stock into the pan and bring to the boil, then reduce the heat and simmer gently for about 15 minutes until the liquid has slightly reduced and the vegetables are completely tender.

Heat a griddle pan and cook the sausages for 10-15 minutes until cooked through and well marked.

Drain the potatoes in a colander and then peel while they are still hot. Push through a potato ricer or sieve using a spatula. Quickly heat the milk in a pan. Beat the butter into the warm mashed potato and then add enough milk to make a smooth but firm purée. Season to taste.

TO SERVE, using two tablespoons, shape the potato purée into quenelles and arrange two in each warmed wide-rimmed serving bowl. Spoon around the bacon and vegetable mixture. Cut the sausages on the diagonal and arrange on top. Scatter over the thyme leaves to garnish.

THE TRADITIONAL BUTCHER

I am keen to use meat reared locally and prepared in the traditional way because I really appreciate the skills of craft butchers. I don't have far to go. In the busy village of Wellington Bridge, a few miles down the road from Dunbrody, Leo Halford is a traditional family butcher who doesn't try to rush things, hanging meat until it is really tender and the flavour has fully developed. He's always happy to cut and prepare meat to suit the dishes we plan to put on the menu at Dunbrody. In Ireland we trace meat from farm to fork. Leo really does know where his meat is coming from; for instance, that the lamb Leo is selling this week came from his own farm. I use it in a Dunbrody speciality, *Roast rack of lamb in an Irish stew consommé* (page 88).

One of Leo's other suppliers for beef would be Tommy Drought, who grazes his cattle in the Dunbrody estate. Grass-fed cattle, like Irish lamb, has great flavour and the temperate climate of Ireland allows cattle to graze naturally on the green pastures of Ireland almost all year round. Even when housed for a couple of months in the depths of the winter they are normally fed natural grass fodder. The dairy industry in Ireland dictates that the main source of calves bred for beef production is from the national cow herd, and these are cross-bred cattle of a type common throughout Ireland, late-maturing beef from Limousin bulls on Fresian cows. Early-maturing beef is usually bred from Irish Hereford, Irish Angus and sometimes Shorthorn sires.

Desserts

BAILEYS CREAM POTS WITH SHORTBREAD BISCUITS 114

IRISH CREAM PUDDING,
WITH FRESH AUTUMN BLISS RASPBERRIES 117

RHUBARB JELLY WITH RHUBARB COMPÔTE 118

BREAD AND BUTTER PUDDING WITH IRISH MIST 121

POACHED PEARS WITH 'RAGLAN ROAD' RICE PUDDING 122

IRISH WHISKEY CHOCOLATE FONDANT 125

WEXFORD STRAWBERRY AND APPLE CRUMBLE 126

ORANGE SCENTED PASTRY CAGE WITH FRESH BERRIES AND
GRAND MARNIER ICE CREAM 129

DUNBRODY KISS 132

Desserts

WEXFORD STRAWBERRIES

Travelling through County Wexford in high summer you cannot miss the roadside stalls of local fruit growers selling strawberries and other summer fruits. Strawberries are an indigenous fruit grown all over the island but, by common consent, the climate of the sunny south-east and the particular qualities of its soil combine with the expertise of families with generations of experience in growing soft fruits to produce the most flavoursome strawberries in the country.

We grow our own strawberries and soft fruits in the kitchen gardens at Dunbrody but like everyone else in Ireland I can't resist shopping at roadside stalls - You can't beat biting into a freshly picked strawberry. The coast of Wexford is a favourite holiday destination for Dubliners and part of the ritual of Summer is pulling in at the roadside to buy strawberries to eat in the car and maybe a few more punnets to enjoy for dessert, such as my *Wexford strawberry and apple crumble* (page126).

BAILEYS CREAM POTS WITH SHORTBREAD BISCUITS

THESE BAILEYS CREAM POTS LITERALLY TAKE MINUTES TO PREPARE. JUST BE CAREFUL TO WHIP YOUR CREAM LIGHTLY, AS THE ALCOHOL IN THE BAILEYS WILL SLIGHTLY THICKEN IT ANYWAY. THE SHORTBREAD WILL KEEP WELL IN AN AIRTIGHT CONTAINER FOR UP TO ONE WEEK, AND IS JUST THE THING WITH A CUP OF MORNING COFFEE.

300ml/½ pint/1⅓ cups cream

4 tbsp/5 US tablespoons Baileys Irish cream

50ml/2fl oz/¼ cup freshly brewed espresso, cooled (1 shot)

250g/9oz carton mascarpone cheese

2 tbsp/2½ US tablespoons sifted icing sugar, plus extra for dusting

cocoa powder, for dusting

FOR THE SHORTBREAD BISCUITS

175g/6oz/1½ cups plain flour, plus a little extra

pinch salt

100g/4oz/1 stick butter (at room temperature)

50g/2oz/¼ cup caster sugar

1 egg

chocolate curls (page 164) and spun-sugar corkscrews (page 163), to decorate

Serves 4

Whip the cream in a bowl until soft peaks have formed. Place the Baileys Irish cream in a bowl with the espresso, mascarpone cheese and icing sugar. Beat until well combined, then fold in the cream. Divide between 4 x 200ml/7fl oz/1 scant cup ramekins or cups and chill for at least 2 hours, or overnight if convenient.

TO MAKE THE SHORTBREAD BISCUITS, preheat the oven to 180°C/350°F/Gas 4. Sift the flour and salt into a bowl and set aside. Cream the butter and sugar in a separate bowl until pale and fluffy. Slowly beat in the egg and then work in the sifted flour until you have achieved a fairly soft dough.

Knead the dough lightly on a lightly floured work surface, then roll out to a 0.5cm/¼in thickness. Using a heart-shaped cutter, stamp out biscuits, and then arrange them on non-stick baking sheets. Bake for 8-10 minutes until cooked through and lightly golden. Leave to cool for 5 minutes, then transfer to a wire rack and leave to cool completely.

TO SERVE, arrange the Baileys cream pots on serving plates and decorate with chocolate curls and spun-sugar corkscrews. Add the shortbread biscuits and dust lightly with the icing sugar and cocoa powder.

IRISH CREAM PUDDING WITH FRESH AUTUMN BLISS RASPBERRIES

THE BEAUTY OF THIS DESSERT IS THAT IT IS SMOOTH, SILKY AND RICH. FOR THE SWEETER TOOTH, TRY DRIZZLING OVER A LITTLE HONEY TO SERVE. IT'S IDEAL FOR A DINNER PARTY AS YOU CAN MAKE THE CREAM PUDDINGS THE DAY BEFORE AND KEEP THEM IN THE FRIDGE UNTIL NEEDED. WET THE SERVING PLATES WITH A TRICKLE OF COLD WATER SO YOU CAN SLIDE THE CREAM PUDDINGS INTO POSITION, THEN WIPE THE EXCESS WATER OFF WITH KITCHEN PAPER. GELATINE LEAVES ARE USED HERE, BUT YOU COULD ALSO USE POWDERED GELATINE IF PREFERRED: IT IS SOLD IN SACHETS OF 11G/0.4 OZ (3 LEVEL TEASPOONS), WHICH IS USUALLY ENOUGH TO SET ABOUT 600ML/1 PINT/2 ¾ CUPS OF LIQUID WHEN CHILLED; INSTRUCTIONS ARE GIVEN ON THE PACK.

300ml/½ pint/1⅓ cups double cream

75ml/3fl oz/⅓ cup milk

2 gelatine leaves

50g/2oz/¼ cup sugar

2 tbsp/2½ US tablespoons light rum

12 raspberries

pouring cream, to serve

Serves 4

Place the cream and milk in a pan and bring slowly to the boil. When the liquid starts to creep up the sides of the pan, adjust the heat so that it maintains a medium boil and continue to cook for a good 5 minutes, until slightly reduced.

Meanwhile, place the gelatine leaves in a bowl of cold water to soak for 10 minutes until they soften.

Stir the sugar into the reduced cream mixture with the rum and allow to dissolve. Remove from the heat and leave to cool for a few seconds. Drain the gelatine leaves and gently squeeze dry. Add to the pan and whisk continuously until dissolved. Leave to cool.

Divide the mixture equally between 4 x 120ml/4fl oz/½ cup dariole moulds or ramekins. Place on a baking sheet and leave them to set in the fridge for at least 3 hours. (They can be left in the fridge for up to two days, if required.)

TO SERVE, dip the dariole moulds into hot water for a few seconds, then gently pull the pudding away from the sides of the mould with a small palette knife. Invert and gently shake out on to serving plates. Arrange three of the raspberries on each plate to decorate and drizzle a little of the pouring cream over each one.

RHUBARB JELLY WITH RHUBARB COMPÔTE

THESE LOVELY TRANSLUCENT JELLIES NOT ONLY LOOK STUNNING BUT ARE
REALLY REFRESHING TOO. WE FIND THAT THIS IS A GREAT WAY TO TURN A
GLUT OF EARLY SUMMER PRODUCE IN THE DUNBRODY KITCHEN GARDEN
TO ADVANTAGE - THEY ARE EXCELLENT THIRST-QUENCHERS ON HOT DAYS
AND THE CHAMPAGNE GIVES THEM A SURPRISING PUNCH.

FOR THE RHUBARB JELLY

225g/8oz rhubarb, trimmed and chopped

225g/8oz strawberries, hulled,
and halved if large

250g/9oz sugar

juice of 1 lemon

6 gelatine leaves (or use powered gelatine,
see introduction page 117)

½ bottle champagne
(375ml/13fl oz/1¾ cups)

FOR THE RHUBARB COMPÔTE

225g/8oz rhubarb, trimmed and
cut into 2.5cm/1in pieces

100g/4oz/½ cup sugar

1 tbsp/1¼ US tablespoons
Grand Marnier

crème fraîche, to serve

Serves 4

TO MAKE THE RHUBARD JELLY, place the rhubarb and strawberries in a metal bowl with the sugar and lemon juice. Cover tightly with cling film, ensuring there is an airtight seal, and set over a pan of simmering water for 20 minutes, until the sugar has completely dissolved and all of the juice has come out of the fruit.

Meanwhile, place the gelatine in a bowl of cold water and set aside for 10 minutes. Drain and gently squeeze dry. Place in a small pan with a little of the juice that has come out of the fruits, and heat gently until dissolved.

Strain the remaining warmed fruit mixture through a fine sieve, into a large jug. Pour in the champagne, then stir in the dissolved gelatine mixture. Pour into 4 x 120ml/4fl oz/½ cup timbales and place in the fridge for at least 4 hours, or preferably overnight, to set. These will keep happily in the fridge for up to two days.

TO MAKE THE RHUBARB COMPÔTE, place the rhubarb in a pan with the sugar and Grand Marnier. Bring to the boil, then reduce the heat and simmer gently for about 10 minutes until the rhubarb is completely tender but still holding its shape. Remove from the heat and leave to cool completely. Transfer to a plastic container with a lid and keep in the fridge, for up to two days.

TO SERVE, spoon the rhubarb compôte into wide-rimmed serving bowls and allow to come back up to room temperature. Dip the jellies briefly in hot water, then invert onto the compôte. Add a dollop of crème fraîche to each one.

THIS IS A PUDDING THAT CAN BE MADE IN SO MANY DIFFERENT WAYS. I PERSONALLY PREFER THIS CLASSIC SOFT SET, WITH ITS WONDERFUL BUTTERY TOP. IT IS ALSO FABULOUS MADE WITH DAY-OLD BRIOCHE OR CROISSANTS INSTEAD OF THE TRADITIONAL WHITE SLICED PAN. AND THE IRISH MIST CAN BE REPLACED WITH ANY OTHER APPROPRIATE LIQUEUR – SHERIDANS, FOR EXAMPLE - OR OMITTED ALTOGETHER IF PREFERRED.

121

BREAD AND BUTTER PUDDING WITH IRISH MIST

50g/2oz raisins

2 tbsp/2 1/2 US tablespoons Irish Mist

75g/3oz/3/4 stick butter (at room temperature)

12 slices medium-sliced white bread

300ml/1/2 pint/1 1/3 cups cream

300ml/1/2 pint/1 1/3 cups milk

4 egg yolks

75g/3oz/1/3 cup caster sugar

2 eggs

butterscotch sauce (page 162) and custard (page 163), to serve

Serves 4

Place the raisins in a small bowl with the Irish Mist and leave to soak for about 2 hours, or overnight, until the raisins have absorbed the liqueur and plumped up. Drain off any excess liquid before using.

Generously butter an ovenproof dish (approximately 1 litre/1 3/4 pint/ 4 1/2 cups in capacity). Remove the crusts from the bread and, using the remaining butter, butter both sides, then cut each slice into quarters.

Arrange a single layer of the bread triangles, slightly overlapping in the bottom of the buttered dish. Scatter over some of the drained raisins and place another layer of the bread triangles on top and scatter over the remaining raisins. Press down gently with a fish slice or spatula.

To make the custard, heat the cream and milk in a pan until it almost comes to the boil. Remove from the heat. Meanwhile, whisk together the egg yolks and sugar in a large heatproof bowl set over a pan of simmering water until thickened and the whisk leaves a trail in the mixture. Remove from the heat and beat in the cream mixture until well combined.

Pour two-thirds of the custard over the layered-up bread triangles and leave to stand for about 30 minutes, or until the bread has soaked up all of the custard.

Preheat the oven to 180°C/350°F/Gas 4. Pour the remaining custard over the soaked bread and butter triangles and arrange the rest of the bread triangles on top. Press down firmly with a fish slice so that the custard comes halfway up the bread triangles. Bake for 30-35 minutes until the custard is just set and the top is golden brown.

TO SERVE, bring the bread and butter pudding straight to the table and have separate jugs of the butterscotch sauce and custard to hand around so that everyone can help themselves.

POACHED PEARS WITH 'RAGLAN ROAD' RICE PUDDING

RICE PUDDING BRINGS BACK MEMORIES OF CHILDHOOD, ALTHOUGH THIS DESSERT IS A LITTLE MORE SOPHISTICATED THAN THE VERSION I WOULD HAVE ENJOYED THEN. THE PEARS IMPROVE WITH KEEPING, MAKING THIS AN EXCELLENT DESSERT FOR ENTERTAINING.

FOR THE POACHED PEARS

4 firm, ripe pears

1 small lemon, cut into quarters

1 small orange, cut into quarters

250g/9oz/1 cup plus 2 US tablespoons caster sugar

500ml/18fl oz/2 ¼ cups red wine

FOR THE RICE PUDDING

300ml/ ½ pint/1 ⅓ cups milk

150ml/ ¼ pint/ ⅔ cup cream

50g/2oz short-grain pudding rice

25g/1oz/ ¼ stick butter

40g/1½ oz/3 US tablespoons caster sugar

½ vanilla pod, split and seeds scraped out, plus 4 extra to decorate

knob of butter

Serves 4

TO POACH THE PEARS, peel the pears, leaving the stalks in place and remove the cores. Stand them upright in a pan that fits them comfortably and add the lemon, orange, sugar and wine. Add a little water if the pears are not completely covered in liquid and bring to a simmer, then cook gently for 40-45 minutes until completely tender. Remove from the heat and leave to cool in the liquid for at least 2 hours or the next day is best to allow the flavours to infuse.

To make the rice pudding, place the milk in a pan with the cream and bring to a simmer. Stir in the rice, butter, sugar and vanilla seeds and bring to the boil, stirring until the sugar has dissolved. Reduce the heat to the lowest setting and cook for 45 minutes or until the rice is tender and creamy, stirring frequently.

When ready to serve, drain the poaching liquid from the pears into a small pan and reduce by half or until thickened and syrupy.

TO SERVE, fan out the pears, leaving the stalks intact and arrange on serving plates. Drizzle a little of the reduced syrup over each one. Dip two tablespoons into hot water and use to shape the rice pudding into large quenelles. Place one on each serving plate and drizzle over a little of the reduced syrup - the remainder can be served in a small jug separately. Decorate with the vanilla pods.

IRISH WHISKEY CHOCOLATE FONDANT

THESE CHOCOLATE PUDDINGS ARE VERY RICH AND VERY MOREISH. GOOD QUALITY CHOCOLATE MAKES ALL THE DIFFERENCE, SO TRY TO GET CHOCOLATE WITH A MINIMUM OF 50% COCOA SOLIDS.

100g/4oz/1 stick butter

200g/7oz plain chocolate, broken into pieces

2 tbsp/2 ½ US tablespoons Jameson whiskey

3 eggs, separated

100g/4oz/½ cup caster sugar

pouring cream, to serve

Serves 4

Preheat the oven to 180°C/350°F/Gas 4. Generously butter 4 x heatproof cups or ramekins that are approximately 7.5cm/3in in diameter and 4cm/1½in deep, using 25g/1oz/¼ stick of the butter. Melt the chocolate in a heatproof bowl set over a pan of simmering water. Remove from the heat and whisk in the remaining 75g/3oz/¾ stick of butter until melted. Stir in the whiskey and set aside to cool.

Place the egg whites in a bowl and whisk until stiff peaks have formed. Whisk in half of the sugar, a third at a time, whisking well after each addition until stiff and very shiny.

In a separate bowl, beat the remaining sugar and egg yolks until pale and fluffy, then beat into the cooled chocolate mixture. Fold in the meringue and use to fill the prepared cups two-thirds full. Arrange on a baking sheet and bake for 12 minutes until well risen but still with a slight wobble in the middle.

TO SERVE, arrange the Irish whiskey chocolate fondants on serving plates, with small jugs of pouring cream.

REPLACE THE APPLES WITH RHUBARB OR BLACKBERRIES IF YOU'D PREFER. THE CRUMBLE MIXTURE WORKS REALLY WELL ON TOP OF ANY FRUIT AND THE DARK MUSCOVADO, TOGETHER WITH BLANCHED ALMONDS (A POPULAR INGREDIENT IN IRISH COOKERY SINCE THE 18TH CENTURY) AND PINHEAD OATMEAL GIVE IT THAT CLASSIC CRUNCHINESS.

WEXFORD STRAWBERRY AND APPLE CRUMBLE

300g/11oz sugar pastry (page 164)

1 egg yolk beaten with 2 tbsp/ 2 1/2 US tablespoons water

225g/8oz apples, peeled, cored and cut into slices (such as Granny Smith or Coxes)

225g/8oz strawberries, hulled and halved if large

40g/1 1/2 oz/3 US tablespoons caster sugar

finely grated rind and juice of 1 small orange

25g/1oz/2 US tablespoons plain flour

25g/1oz/2 US tablespoons wholemeal flour

1/4 tsp baking powder

25g/1oz/2 US tablespoons dark muscovado sugar

25g/1oz blanched almonds, finely chopped

1 tsp fine pinhead oatmeal

25g/1oz/1/4 stick butter, cut into cubes

crème fraîche, to serve

Serves 6

Divide the sugar pastry into six pieces and use to line 6 x 10cm/4in individual tartlet tins that are 4cm/1 1/2in deep. As this pastry is so short you may find it easier to press it into the tins in an even layer, using the tips of your fingers rather than rolling out. Arrange on a large baking sheet and chill for at least 15 minutes to allow the pastry to rest.

Preheat the oven to 180°C/350°F/Gas 4. Line each pastry case with a circle of non-stick parchment paper that is first crumpled up to make it easier to handle. Fill with baking beans or dried pulses and bake for about 15 minutes until the pastry cases look 'set', but not coloured.

Carefully remove the paper from the pastry cases, then brush the insides with the egg wash to form a seal. Place in the oven for another 5 minutes or until the bases are firm to the touch and the sides are lightly coloured. Remove from the oven and leave until cool enough to handle, then carefully take out of the tins and leave to cool completely on a wire rack.

Reduce the oven temperature to 160°C/325°F/Gas 3. Place the apples and strawberries in a pan with the caster sugar, orange rind and juice. Bring to a simmer, then cover and cook gently for 5 minutes until the fruits are tender but still holding their shape. Remove from the heat and leave to cool.

Sift the plain and wholemeal flour into a bowl with the baking powder, then tip the residue from the sieve back into the bowl. Stir in the muscovado sugar, almonds and oatmeal. Rub in the butter until the mixture resembles breadcrumbs. Divide the cooled fruit mixture among the pastry cases and sprinkle the crumble on top. Arrange on a large baking sheet and bake for another 20-25 minutes until the crumble topping is crisp and golden brown.

TO SERVE, arrange the crumbles on serving plates (warm or cold) and, using two dessertspoons dipped in hot water, add a quenelle of crème fraîche to each one.

ORANGE SCENTED PASTRY CAGE WITH FRESH BERRIES AND GRAND MARNIER ICE CREAM

THIS RECIPE IS MORE 'BLUE PETER' THAN ACTUAL COOKING BUT THE RESULTS ARE BOUND TO BE A TALKING POINT WITH YOUR GUESTS FOR THE REST OF THE EVENING - REVEAL NOTHING!

4 tbsp/5 US tablespoons lightly whipped cream

50g/2oz mixed berries, such has halved small strawberries, blueberries, blackcurrants and raspberries

4 small scoops Grand Marnier ice cream (page 165)

4 spun-sugar discs (page 163)

4 tbsp/5 US tablespoons mixed berry compôte (page 162)

FOR THE TUILE BISCUITS

50g/2oz/½ stick unsalted butter, softened

100g/4oz/½ cup icing sugar, sifted

finely grated rind of 1 small orange

2 tbsp/2½ US tablespoons honey

100g/4oz egg whites (about 3 large eggs)

100g/4oz/1 scant cup plain flour, sifted

Serves 4

To make the tuile biscuits, cream the butter in a bowl with the sugar and orange rind until pale and fluffy. Slowly add the honey and continue to beat until well mixed, then gradually add the egg whites, beating well after each addition.

Beat the flour into the tuile mixture until thoroughly smooth. Cover with cling film and place in the fridge to rest for at least 1 hour (up to 24 hours is fine).

Preheat the oven to 180°C/350°F/Gas 4. Spoon the tuile mixture into a piping bag with a nozzle that is 0.25cm/⅛in wide. Line two large baking sheets with matts of non-stick silicone or parchment paper. To make each cage, pipe an L shape. (STEP 1) *See overleaf*

Shape each L shape into a boot, then fill each boot shape with trellis and repeat until you have 4 cages in total. Any remaining mixture will freeze very well to use for another time. Bake for 5-6 minutes until just cooked through and lightly coloured. (STEP 2)

Remove from the oven, and working quickly with a palette knife while the biscuits are still hot, gently bend them around a rolling pin into cages, holding until set - just take care not to burn your fingers! (STEP 3) Transfer to a wire rack and leave to cool.

TO SERVE, place the cream in a piping bag with the nozzle that is 0.25cm/⅛in wide. Pipe a little into the middle of each serving plate and use to secure the tuile cages in an upright position, then carefully fill with the berries. Add a scoop of the ice cream on top of each one and decorate with the spun-sugar discs, then spoon around the mixed berry compôte.

THIS IS OUR SIGNATURE DESSERT AT DUNBRODY AND REALLY ISN'T THAT DIFFICULT TO MAKE. IT IS AN INTENSELY CHOCOLATEY EXPERIENCE AND NEVER FAILS TO IMPRESS – JUST MAKE SURE YOU USE THE BEST POSSIBLE QUALITY CHOCOLATE. THERE IS NO DOUBT IN MY MIND THAT THERE IS SOMETHING ABOUT CHOCOLATE THAT IS ADDICTIVE. IT CONTAINS SEVERAL STIMULANTS, INCLUDING CAFFEINE AND PLEASURE-INDUCING ENDORPHINS – NO WONDER IT TASTES SO GOOD!

DUNBRODY KISS

450g/1lb plain chocolate, broken into pieces

5 eggs, separated

600ml/1 pint/2 ¾ cups cream

1 fun size Mars bar, chopped

50g/2oz cornflakes, lightly crushed

FOR THE CHOCOLATE SHARDS

50g/2oz plain chocolate, broken into pieces

50g/2oz white chocolate, broken into pieces

FOR THE CHOCOLATE GANACHE

75g/3oz plain chocolate, broken into pieces

85ml/3fl oz cream, plus a little extra if neccessary

handful small halved strawberries and raspberries, to decorate

Select 6 x 200ml / 7fl oz / 1 scant cup in capacity teacups and line them with cling film. Melt the plain chocolate in a heatproof bowl set over a pan of simmering water. Leave to cool a little. Lightly beat the egg yolks, then whisk into the melted chocolate. Whip the cream in a bowl until you have achieved soft peaks, then whisk into the chocolate mixture.

In a separate bowl, beat the egg whites until stiff, then fold into the chocolate mixture. Divide among the lined teacups and chill for at least 2 hours or, preferably, overnight. When the chocolate mousse has set, melt the Mars bar in a small pan. Remove from the heat and fold in the cornflakes. Leave to cool a little, then add a layer to each chocolate mousse to form a crunchy base. Place in the freezer for at least 2 hours; (up to one month is fine, if required).

TO MAKE THE CHOCOLATE SHARDS, melt both chocolates in heat-proof bowls set over pans of simmering water. Line a baking sheet with cling film. Spoon on blobs of both chocolates and then cover with cling film. Gently roll to form one even layer. Place in the freezer for at least 10 minutes (or for up to one month, if required).

TO MAKE THE CHOCOLATE GANACHE, heat the chocolate and cream for 1-2 minutes until melted, stirring constantly. The consistency should coat the back of a wooden spoon. If you think it is too thick, add a little more cream. Invert the teacups onto a wire rack set over a clean tray and then carefully peel away the cling film. Ladle a little of the chocolate ganache over each one until completely coated, allowing the excess to drip onto the tray below. Using a spatula, scrape the excess chocolate ganache into a pan and reheat gently. Leave to a cool a little.

TO SERVE, using a fish slice, transfer the coated chocolate mousses on to serving plates and leave to defrost at room temperature for 10 minutes, then decorate with the strawberries and raspberries and drizzle around the cooled chocolate ganache. Now, working quickly, remove the sheet of chocolate shards from the freezer and peel away the cling film, then break into shards and stick two into the top of each Dunbrody Kiss.

Kitchen Garden

CHAMP 140

MUM'S ROAST POTATOES 140

WARM NEW POTATO SALAD 141

STEAMED BABY NEW POTATOES 141

CRUSHED CARROTS AND PARSNIPS 142

BRAISED FENNEL 142

ROASTED VEGETABLE SALAD 143

DUNBRODY CUCUMBER PICKLE WITH ROCKET 144

HONEY-GLAZED CARROTS 145

BUTTERED CURLY KALE 145

BUTTERED ASPARAGUS WITH HOLLANDAISE SAUCE 146

HOOK HEAD POTATOES

Potatoes are essential in many Irish dishes - and it's not the case that any old spud will do. The way potatoes are traditionally used in Irish dishes often demands a floury potato, one of the many varieties grown throughout Ireland that has a high level of starchy dry matter and a low water content. Almost all the potatoes used at Dunbrody House are grown by specialist growers Vincent and Geraldine Rowe in the townland of Conna, near Fethard-on-Sea on the Hook Head Peninsula.

That address itself tells Irish potato-lovers what they need to know. Potatoes thrive on sandy soil close to the sea and Hook Peninsula also benefits from a micro-climate that is sunny and dry. When Vincent uses a sprong to lift the new season potatoes, the soil is so light and sandy it runs freely through his fingers, leaving the tender skin of the new potatoes unblemished. Food-lovers in Ireland believe there is nothing to beat the flavour of a freshly-dug new potato and eagerly await the new season; but they still demand them to be floury and that takes a very high degree of skill.

The craft of growing top class potatoes has been passed down through four generations of the Rowe family and luckily Vincent is willing to share his knowledge with me. "Every year we take fresh ground to grow them rather than using our own land. We plant as early as February, devoting about ten acres to the early varieties. Our aim is to get the potatoes as floury as we can and British Queens are the best of the early varieties - they easily grow large and floury right next to the sea. The finest main crop variety is *Golden Wonder*, although we do grow *Roosters* as well. You must wait until the potatoes are mature and ready for eating, so we pick first earlies as the flowers go off. Hand-digging is best while the skins are soft; as they begin to get a little harder we use a small chain digger and, after about three weeks, we can use the main potato harvester. Potatoes should be stored at all times in the dark, in dry, cool (but not cold) conditions." As we all agree, 'laughing potatoes', so called because when the skin splits during cooking they look as of they are smiling, should always be steamed not boiled in case they collapse into mush in the pot.

CHAMP

CHAMP IS A TRADITIONAL IRISH POTATO DISH THAT HAS RECENTLY ENJOYED A RENAISSANCE IN CONTEMPORARY COOKING. IT SHOULD BE SOFT IN CONSISTENCY BUT NOT SLOPPY. ONCE MASTERED, THIS RECIPE CAN BE ADAPTED FOR DIFFERENT RESULTS. TRY REPLACING THE MILK WITH CRÈME FRAÎCHE OR QUARK (SKIMMED-MILK SOFT CHEESE), OR ADD SOME STEAMED CABBAGE TO TURN IT INTO THAT OTHER IRISH FAVOURITE, COLCANNON.

675g/1½ lb potatoes, well scrubbed

6 tbsp/7½ US tablespoons milk

4 spring onions, finely chopped

50g/2oz/½ stick butter

salt and freshly ground white pepper

Serves 4-6

Cover the potatoes with cold water in a pan and add a pinch of salt. Bring to the boil, then simmer for 15-20 minutes, or until completely tender when pierced with the tip of a sharp knife.

Heat the milk in a pan with the spring onions for 5 minutes, or until the spring onions have softened. Drain the potatoes in a colander, then peel while they are still hot. Push through a potato ricer or sieve, using a spatula. Beat 40g/1½oz of the butter into the warm mashed potato and then mix in the milk and spring onion mixture. Season to taste.

TO SERVE, spoon into a warmed serving dish and make a slight dip in the middle. Add the remaining knob of butter and allow it to melt into the champ.

MUM'S ROAST POTATOES

THIS IS MY MUM'S RECIPE AND IT HAS NEVER FAILED ME. THERE'S NO DOUBT THAT THE FAT FROM THE ROAST MEAT MAKES THE BEST ROAST POTATOES. ALTERNATIVELY, IF YOU EVER ROAST A GOOSE OR DUCK, SAVE EVERY DROP OF THE FAT AND FREEZE IT DOWN IN ICE CUBE TRAYS, THEN BAG IT TO USE AT YOUR LEISURE – EVEN A COUPLE ADDED TO YOUR OIL WILL HELP THE FLAVOUR.

675g/1½ lb floury potatoes cut into large even-sized chunks (such as Rooster or Golden Wonder, preferably all similar in size)

vegetable oil, or dripping, goose or duck fat

Maldon sea salt

Serves 4-6

Preheat the oven to 220°C/425°F/Gas 7. Place the potatoes in a pan of cold salted water and bring to the boil. Reduce the heat, cover and simmer for 8-10 minutes, until the outsides have just softened. Drain and return to the pan for a minute or two, to dry out.

Meanwhile, preheat a roasting tin with a 1cm/½in of oil, or dripping, goose or duck fat, for a few minutes until just smoking. Put the lid back on the potatoes and shake vigorously to break up and soften the edges or roughly prod the outside of the potatoes with a fork. Carefully tip them into the hot oil, basting the tops.

Place the roasting tin with the potatoes back in the oven and cook for 40 minutes, then pour off the majority of the fat before turning the potatoes over. Season to taste with the salt and cook for a further 20 minutes until crispy around the edges and golden brown.

TO SERVE, tip the roast potatoes into a warmed serving dish.

WARM NEW POTATO SALAD

675g/1½ lb small new potatoes, scraped or scrubbed and halved if large

1 tsp white wine vinegar

1 tbsp/1¼ US tablespoons olive oil

4 tbsp/5 US tablespoons mayonnaise

2 tsp wholegrain mustard

4 spring onions, thinly sliced

1 tbsp/1¼ US tablespoons chopped fresh tarragon

salt and freshly ground black pepper

Serves 4-6

THIS IS A CLASSIC RECIPE THAT IS ESSENTIAL AT ANY BARBECUE OR PICNIC AT THE DUNDON HOUSEHOLD. IT'S REALLY GOOD IF YOU STIR IN A COUPLE OF SPOONFULS OF MY DUNBRODY CUCUMBER PICKLE (PAGE 144) THAT HAS BEEN DRAINED OF EXCESS LIQUID. TRY SERVING IT WITH SOME POACHED SPRING SALMON: YOU'LL BE IN HEAVEN!

Place the potatoes in a pan of salted water, bring to the boil and cook for 12-15 minutes or until tender. This will depend on your potatoes, so keep an eye on them.

Meanwhile, whisk together the white wine vinegar in a small bowl with the olive oil and season to taste. Drain the potatoes well, transfer to a serving bowl and gently stir in the dressing. Leave to cool completely.

Stir the mayonnaise and wholegrain mustard together in a small bowl and stir into the potatoes with the spring onions and tarragon. Season to taste.

TO SERVE, tip the potato salad into a serving bowl.

STEAMED BABY NEW POTATOES

CHOOSE. SMALL. EVEN-SIZED NEW POTATOES FOR THIS RECIPE. FOR ME. NOTHING CAN BEAT THE PLEASURE OF COOKING MY FIRST BATCH OF NEW SEASON HOOK POTATOES. THEY SHOULD BE BOUGHT IN SMALL QUANTITIES. AS NEW POTATOES KEPT HANGING AROUND MAY LOOK FINE. BUT THEY WILL HAVE AN UNPLEASANT MOULDY TASTE WHEN EATEN.

675g/1½ lb small new potatoes, scraped or scrubbed clean

2 large fresh mint sprigs

knob of butter

Maldon sea salt

Serves 4-6

Place the potatoes in a steamer set over a pan of cold water and add a pinch of salt. Bring to the boil and then steam for 10 minutes.

Add one of the sprigs of mint and continue to cook for a further 2-5 minutes or until the potatoes are tender when pierced with a small sharp knife. This will all depend on the size of your potatoes.

TO SERVE, finely chop the leaves from the remaining mint sprig. Drain the potatoes and return them to the pan with the butter and chopped mint. Toss briefly until the butter has melted, then tip into a warmed serving dish and season with salt.

CRUSHED CARROTS AND PARSNIPS

THE NATURAL SWEETNESS OF THE CARROTS AND PARSNIPS MAKE THIS THE PERFECT ACCOMPANIMENT FOR MY LOIN OF BACON WITH AN IRISH MIST GLAZE (PAGE 92). IT IS THE KIND OF TEXTURED MASH THAT YOU SEE IN RESTAURANTS; SO DON'T BE TEMPTED TO MAKE IT TOO SMOOTH.

4 tbsp/5 US tablespoons olive oil

225g/8oz carrots, cut into chunks

225g/8oz parsnips, quartered, cored and cut into chunks

½ tsp chopped fresh rosemary

salt and freshly ground black pepper

Serves 4

Preheat the oven to 180°C/350°F/Gas 4. Place two tablespoons of the oil in a large roasting tin and add the carrots and parsnips.

Sprinkle the rosemary over the root vegetables and toss everything together until well coated. Season generously. Roast for 40-50 minutes until the vegetables are just beginning to catch and caramelise around the edges.

Remove the roasted carrots and parsnips from the oven and add the remaining olive oil, then crush with a potato masher until roughly mashed. Season to taste.

TO SERVE, spoon the crushed carrots and parsnips into a warmed dish.

BRAISED FENNEL

FENNEL JUST SEEMS TO GET FORGOTTEN ABOUT ALL TOO OFTEN. ITS DISTINCT FLAVOUR IS PERFECT WITH CHICKEN OR FISH.

4 fennel bulbs

120ml/4fl oz/½ cup olive oil

1 small onion, thinly sliced

3 garlic cloves, finely chopped

1 fresh thyme sprig

1 fresh rosemary sprig

juice of 1 lemon

about 600ml/1 pint/2 ¾ cups kitchen garden vegetable stock (page 168) or water

a little freshly grated Parmesan (optional)

salt and freshly ground black pepper

Serves 4-8

Preheat the oven to 180°C/350°F/Gas 4. Trim the fennel and cut in half, leaving the roots intact. Heat the oil in a casserole dish with a lid and sauté the onion and garlic for 2-3 minutes until softened but not coloured. Stir in the herbs and lemon juice and then season to taste.

Add the fennel pieces to the casserole dish and then pour in enough stock or water to just cover. Season to taste. Cover with a cartouche (a circle of greaseproof paper cut the same diameter as the casserole dish with a small hole in the middle to let the steam escape). Bring to the boil, then transfer to the oven and braise for 35-40 minutes until the fennel is completely tender and lightly glazed.

Remove the fennel from the oven and leave to cool completely in the remaining braising liquid in the casserole dish. Once cold, transfer to a Kilner jar and pour in enough of the braising liquid to cover completely. This will keep happily in the fridge for up to 1 week.

TO SERVE, drain the fennel pieces and either gratinate under the grill sprinkled with a little Parmesan if liked or barbecue over medium coals for about 5 minutes or until warmed through.

ROASTED VEGETABLE SALAD

THIS ROASTED VEGETABLE SALAD IS GREAT ON ITS OWN, OR SERVE AS PART OF A BARBECUE. YOU COULD ALSO TRY ADDING SOME PARMESAN SHAVINGS, OR CHUNKS OF FETA OR GOAT'S CHEESE FOR AN EXTRA DIMENSION. IT WILL KEEP HAPPILY IN THE FRIDGE FOR THREE TO FOUR DAYS.

2 aubergines

3 red peppers

3 green peppers

1 red onion, quartered (skin on)

1 garlic bulb

1 ripe plum tomato

5 tbsp/6 ¼ US tablespoons olive oil

good pinch chopped fresh rosemary

good pinch chopped fresh thyme

1 tbsp/1 ¼ US tablespoons white wine vinegar

1 tbsp/1 ¼ US tablespoons chopped fresh flat-leaf parsley

salt and freshly ground black pepper

Serves 4-6

Preheat the grill or a barbecue. Prick the aubergines all over and place them on a grill rack under the grill or on the barbecue with the peppers, onion, garlic and tomato. Drizzle over two tablespoons of the olive oil and sprinkle over the rosemary and thyme. Season to taste and cook for 10-20 minutes until tender and the skins are blackened and blistered, turning regularly. You'll find that the vegetables all take different times to cook so just use your judgement, making sure that you remove the tomato as soon as the skin splits.

Transfer the vegetables as they are cooked to a shallow non-metallic dish and cover tightly with cling film. This will help to steam off the skins. When they are cool enough to handle, rub or peel off the skins. Tear or chop the aubergines into strips, discarding the stalks. Remove the stems from the peppers and discard the seeds, then tear or chop into strips. Cut the onion into thin wedges and sliver some or all of the garlic cloves. Cut the tomato into wedges.

Combine all of the prepared roasted vegetables in a large bowl and add the remaining oil with the vinegar and parsley. Season to taste and stir gently to combine. Either use immediately or chill covered with cling film until ready to use, just make sure you give it time to come back up to room temperature first.

TO SERVE, spoon the roasted vegetable salad onto serving plates.

DUNBRODY CUCUMBER PICKLE WITH ROCKET

THIS CUCUMBER PICKLE CAN BE USED IN SO MANY DIFFERENT WAYS. IF IT IS STORED IN STERILIZED JARS IT WILL LAST FOR UP TO TWO MONTHS. I FIND IT A USEFUL STAPLE TO KEEP IN THE FRIDGE AS IT IS DELICIOUS ON ITS OWN AS AN APPETISER, WITH PAN-FRIED FISH OR ON A SMOKED SALMON PLATTER...I COULD GO ON AND ON. IT IS ALSO GREAT FOR USING UP THE GLUT OF CUCUMBERS THAT THE SUMMER ALWAYS SEEMS TO BRING.

1 cucumber

1 onion, thinly sliced

2 red chillies, seeded and cut into very fine julienne (slices)

500ml/18fl oz/2 ¼ cups rice wine vinegar

300g/11oz/1 ½ cups light muscovado sugar

2 tsp coriander seeds

good pinch saffron stands

1 tsp Maldon sea salt

100g/4oz rocket

olive oil, for dressing

Serves 4-6

Cut the cucumber in half lengthways and, using a teaspoon, remove the seeds. Using a vegetable peeler, pare the flesh into wafer-thin ribbons and place in a pan. Add the onion, chillies, rice wine vinegar, sugar, coriander seeds, saffron and salt. Slowly bring to the boil, then reduce the heat and simmer for 20 minutes, until the vegetables are completely tender and the liquid has reduced and thickened slightly. If you are not planning to use the cucumber pickle immediately, store in sterilised jars.

TO STERILISE, wash a Kilner jar or a couple of jam jars, rinse thoroughly, then dry in a warm oven. Stand them upside down on a clean tea towel.

If you are using jam jars, fill them, then cover with a disc of waxed paper while still hot or else completely cold, then seal with a dampened disc of clear plastic, secure with an elastic band and screw back on their tops. Simply secure and close a Kilner jar in the normal way. Label and store in a cool, dark place for up to two months, then use as required. Otherwise transfer the cucumber pickle to a bowl, cover with cling film and chill until needed.

TO SERVE, drain the excess liquid from the cucumber pickle and fold in the rocket leaves, then lightly dress with olive oil. Arrange on serving plates.

HONEY-GLAZED CARROTS

THIS IS MY VERSION OF VICHY-STYLE CARROTS, WHICH ARE TRADITIONALLY COOKED IN WATER FROM THE FAMOUS SPA. WHEN COOKING, MAKE SURE YOU SHAKE THE PAN OCCASIONALLY TO PREVENT THE BOTTOM CATCHING AND THE GLAZE CARAMELIZING. I FIND THAT THEY REHEAT VERY WELL SO CAN BE MADE WELL IN ADVANCE AND JUST POPPED INTO THE MICROWAVE OR STIRRED IN A PAN UNTIL WARMED THROUGH.

450g/1lb carrots, thinly sliced on the diagonal

25g/1oz/¼ stick butter

1 tbsp/1¼ US tablespoons honey

about 300ml/½ pint kitchen garden vegetable stock (page 168) or water

1 tsp sesame seeds

salt and freshly ground black pepper

Serves 4

Place the carrots in a small pan with the butter, honey and enough stock or water to just cover the carrots. Bring to the boil, then cook over a moderate to high heat for about 12 minutes, until the carrots are tender and all of the liquid has evaporated, shaking the pan occasionally to prevent sticking.

Meanwhile, toast the sesame seeds in a heavy-based frying pan. Tip on to a plate and leave to cool. When the carrots are cooked, tip in the sesame seeds and toss until evenly coated. Season to taste.

TO SERVE, spoon the honey-glazed carrots into a warmed serving dish.

BUTTERED CURLY KALE

THIS IS A VERY SIMPLE RECIPE AND ONE OF MY FAVOURITE WAYS OF PREPARING CURLY KALE. IF YOU WANT TO RING IN THE CHANGES, YOU COULD TRY SUBSTITUTING SPINACH OR ANY OTHER LEAFY GREEN VEGETABLE, SUCH AS SAVOY CABBAGE, FOR THE CURLY KALE.

1 tbsp/1¼ US tablespoons olive oil

25g/1oz/¼ stick butter

1 shallot, finely chopped

4 tbsp/5 US tablespoons white wine

675g/1½ lb curly kale, thick stalks removed and shredded

salt and freshly ground black pepper

Serves 4–6

Heat the oil in a sauté pan. Add the butter and once it has stopped foaming, tip in the shallot. Sauté for 2-3 minutes until softened but not coloured.

Add the white wine to the pan and allow to bubble up and slightly reduce, then tip in the curly kale and sauté for another 2-3 minutes until the curly kale is tender. Season to taste.

TO SERVE, tip the buttered curly kale into the warmed serving dish.

BUTTERED ASPARAGUS WITH HOLLANDAISE SAUCE

HOLLANDAISE SAUCE SHOULD BE LIGHTLY PIQUANT AND HAVE A SMOOTH POURING CONSISTENCY. IF IT IS TOO THICK, ADD A LITTLE WATER OR VINEGAR. IT IS A SAUCE WHICH CURDLES EASILY. IF THIS BEGINS TO HAPPEN, ADD AN ICE CUBE AND WHISK WELL; THE SAUCE SHOULD COME BACK TOGETHER.

20-30 asparagus spears, trimmed

knob of butter

FOR THE HOLLANDAISE SAUCE

1 tbsp/1 ¼ US tablespoons white wine vinegar

1 tbsp/1 ¼ US tablespoons fresh lemon juice

3 egg yolks

about 100g/4oz/1 stick unsalted butter

salt and freshly ground white pepper

Serves 4-6

TO MAKE THE HOLLANDAISE SAUCE, place the vinegar in a heatproof bowl with the lemon juice and egg yolks and a pinch of salt. Whisk until thoroughly combined, then set the bowl over a pan of simmering water on a low heat and whisk for about 3 minutes until the mixture is thick enough to leave a trail when the whisk is lifted.

Meanwhile, melt the butter in a small pan or in the microwave. Gradually add to the egg yolk mixture, a little at a time, whisking constantly. When approximately 75g/3oz/ ¾ stick has been added, season lightly with salt. If it is still too sharp, add a little more butter. Season to taste and keep warm.

Meanwhile, cook the asparagus spears for 3-6 minutes, depending on their size, in a large pan of boiling water or in a steamer standing in 7.5cm/ 3in of boiling water until just tender. Drain, return to the pan, and quickly toss in the knob of butter.

TO SERVE, tip the asparagus onto a warmed serving plate and spoon over the hollandaise sauce or serve it separately in a warmed jug and allow everyone to help themselves.

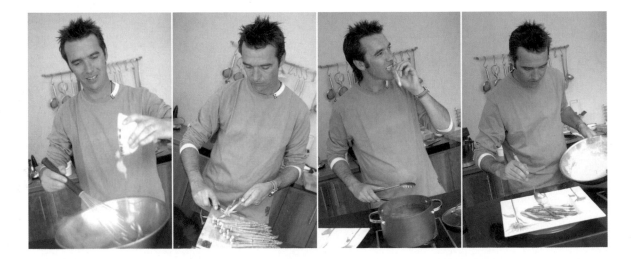

The Larder

DUNBRODY KITCHEN GARDEN

It's fun to 'graze' Irish-style in the kitchen garden, nibbling peas straight from the pod, or crunching on a green bean, then tasting fresh herbs before moving on to the fruit garden to pick juicy strawberries, raspberries, and gooseberries, or plucking a crisp apple or pear from the tree. The gardens at Dunbrody would inspire any chef. Indeed, the team often take a quick early morning trot round the kitchen garden to see what is ready for harvesting. Every day, vegetables, fruit and herbs are picked and brought straight to the kitchen. The variety, flavour and texture of freshly picked, home-grown produce is wonderful.

Although a Georgian country house like Dunbrody would have had a kitchen garden it had disappeared and we had to start from scratch. It was a stroke of fortune that when we began developing the garden (shortly after moving into Dunbrody) internationally renowned gardener, John Seymour, regarded by many aspiring to create a kitchen garden as a guru, had moved from the UK to County Wexford and was teaching people how to grow food organically using traditional methods. The kitchen garden, designed and maintained by head gardener, Michael O'Brien, follows Seymour's basic philosophy that one must work with nature not against it - that the soil should be fed, not the plant. Rather than using artificial fertilisers, deep beds nourished with organic compost provide loose rich soil, encouraging plants to grow downwards, not sideways, thus allowing close planting. As the food crops grow, they crowd out weeds naturally without any need for weed-killers. Growing lots of different plants and, in particular, companion planting discourages harmful insects from attacking the crops, so there is no need for insecticides. Food grown without chemicals tastes as food should.

With an emphasis on varieties of Irish vegetables and fruits that have been traditionally grown all over Ireland for centuries (sometimes for thousands of years) the kitchen, fruit and herb gardens at Dunbrody have inspired me to look at traditional Irish food in order to create contemporary dishes with real Irish character.

IF YOU HAVE A FRIENDLY BAKER AND CAN GET HOLD OF FRESH YEAST, SIMPLY REPLACE THE DRIED SACHETS WITH 25G/1OZ. PLACE IN A SMALL BOWL WITH TWO TABLESPOONS OF WARM WATER (105-115F) AND THEN STIR WITH A FORK UNTIL DISSOLVED. LEAVE TO STAND FOR ABOUT 3 MINUTES BEFORE USING.

CARAMELISED ONION DUNBRODY BREAD

675g/1 ½ lb/6 cups strong white unbleached white flour, plus extra for dusting

2 x 7g/¼ oz sachets easy blend dried yeast, about 1 tbsp in total

about 600ml/1 pint/2 ¾ cups hand-hot water

1 tsp salt

olive oil, for greasing

1 egg beaten with 1 tbsp/1¼ US tablespoons water

2 tbsp/2 ½ US tablespoons onion marmalade (page 158)

butter, to serve

Makes 1 large loaf

Place the flour in the bowl of a food mixer fitted with a dough attachment if you have one. Add the yeast, hand-hot water and salt. Switch on the machine and mix until you have a very sloppy dough. You can also do this by hand and mix with your fingers for 2-3 minutes, then knead to incorporate the flour, scraping the sides of the bowl and folding the dough over itself until it gathers into a rough mass.

Turn the dough out onto a well floured surface; lightly flour your hands. Knead for 6-8 minutes until the dough is smooth and pliable. The dough will be very sticky at first; keep your hands and the work surface lightly floured, using a dough scraper if necessary to prevent it from sticking and building up on the work surface. As you continue kneading, the dough will become more elastic and easier to handle. Shape into a loose ball, then return it to a clean bowl and cover with cling film. Leave to rest for 20 minutes.

Turn the dough out again onto a well floured surface and knead for 2-3 minutes or until it becomes springy and very smooth. Shape into a loose ball and place it in a lightly oiled large bowl. Turn to coat the dough with the oil and cover tightly with cling film. Leave to rise at room temperature for 1 hour, or until it looks slightly puffy but has not doubled in size.

Preheat the oven to 180°C/350°F/Gas 4. Remove the dough from the bowl and form it into an oval shaped loaf. Brush with beaten egg and then spoon the onion marmalade on top. Bake for 45 minutes until the loaf is a deep golden brown and sounds hollow when tapped on the bottom. Transfer to a wire rack and leave to cool before using.

TO SERVE, cut the bread into slices and arrange in a bread basket with a separate pot of butter to serve.

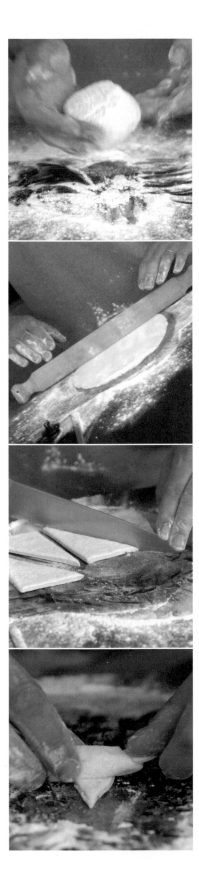

CROSTINI Don't be tempted to make these too far in advance, as the bread goes soggy. Preheat the grill or a griddle pan and use to toast slices of caramelised onion Dunbrody bread, preferably one day old, on both sides. Remove from the heat and immediately rub one side with a halved garlic clove. Drizzle over a little olive oil to finish.

ROLLS Divide the dough into eight to ten pieces. Place on a very lightly floured surface and roll each into a ball or small oval shape. Arrange on a non-stick baking sheet then brush with beaten egg and spoon a teaspoon of the onion marmalade on top of each one. Bake these at 220°C/425°F/ Gas 7 for about 20 minutes.

CROISSANT SHAPED ROLLS Gently roll out the dough to a 1cm/¹/₂ in thickness on a very lightly floured surface and cut into small triangles. Brush with beaten egg and starting at the base of each triangle, roll towards the tip. Shape into half moons and arrange on a non-stick baking sheet with the tips tucked underneath. Bake these at 220°C/425°F/Gas 7 for about 20 minutes.

BREADSTICKS Roll out the dough on a very lightly floured surface into a rectangle that is about 1cm/¹/₂in thick. Brush lightly with olive oil, sprinkle with chopped rosemary or a mixture of freshly chopped herbs, if liked and then sprinkle with Maldon sea salt. Cut into 1cm/¹/₂in strips and place on to a non-stick baking sheet. Bake for 220°C/425°F/Gas 7 10-15 minutes, depending on their size, until crisp and golden brown.

BATONS Divide the dough in half and shape each piece into a long roll with tapering ends, about 35cm/14in long. Transfer to a non-stick large baking sheet and bake these at 180°C/350°F/Gas 4 for about 30 minutes.

FLAVOUR VARIATIONS The dough can be flavoured with a tablespoon of freshly chopped herbs, such as thyme or rosemary or, for a more pronounced taste, add in up to ten tablespoons of chopped fresh mixed herbs, such as flat-leaf parsley, basil and chives. A handful of diced sun-dried tomatoes that have been preserved in oil also works well as would chopped olives; or try adding four tablespoons of sun-dried tomato paste with a teaspoon of fennel seeds.

GLAZING For a deep, golden, shiny finish use the beaten egg mixed with a tablespoon of water as described in the recipe. While egg white gives a pale, shiny glaze; brushing with water gives a crisp crust and milk produces a soft, golden crust. Whole grains, seeds, Maldon sea salt or freshly grated Parmesan can be sprinkled over the dough before baking.

GUINNESS AND PECAN BREAD

450g/1lb/4 cups wholemeal flour

100g/4oz/1 scant cup plain flour, plus extra for dusting

1 tsp bicarbonate of soda

1 tsp salt

50g/2oz rolled oats

50g/2oz pecan halves, roughly chopped

2 eggs

150ml/ ¼ pint/ ⅔ cup Guinness

225ml/8fl oz/1 cup buttermilk, approx.

2 tbsp/2 ½ US tablespoons treacle

sunflower oil, for greasing

Makes 1 loaf

THIS DELICIOUS BREAD IS BEST EATEN AS SOON AS IT IS COOL ENOUGH TO HANDLE. IF YOU WANT TO KEEP IT FOR ANY LONGER, SPRINKLE A LITTLE WATER OVER THE CRUST AS SOON AS IT COMES OUT OF THE OVEN AND WRAP IN A CLEAN TEA TOWEL TO STOP THE CRUST BECOMING TOO HARD.

Preheat the oven to 180°C/350°F/Gas 4. Sieve the wholemeal flour into a bowl with the plain flour, bicarbonate of soda and salt, then tip the residue from the sieve back into the bowl. Stir in the rolled oats and pecan nuts.

Break the eggs into a jug and lightly beat, then stir in the Guinness, buttermilk and treacle, whisking to combine. Make a well in the centre of the dry ingredients and gradually add enough of the egg mixture to mix to a soft but not sloppy dough.

Place in a well oiled 900g/2lb loaf tin and bake for 60 minutes. Run a knife around the tin and ease the bread out. If it sounds hollow when tapped on the bottom it is cooked; if not return it to the oven for another 5-10 minutes. There's no need to put the loaf back in the tin; turn it upside down and put it directly on the shelf. Transfer to a wire rack to cool.

TO SERVE, eat while still warm, cut into slices.

DUNBRODY MARMALADE

THIS UNUSUAL MARMALADE HAS A FRESH LIGHT FLAVOUR AND, AS WELL AS TAKING ITS PLACE AMONG THE MANY TREATS OFFERED FOR THE FAMOUS DUNBRODY BREAKFAST, KEVIN USES IT IN THE KITCHEN AS A GLAZE.

5 oranges

1 grapefruit

250g/9oz/1 cup plus 2 US tablespoons sugar

2 tbsp/2 ½ US tablespoons Irish whiskey

Makes about 1 litre/1 ¾ pints/4 ½ cups

Using a vegetable peeler, thinly pare the rind from one of the oranges and the grapefruit, taking care not to remove the white pith. Cut into very fine shreds and place in a heavy-based pan. Using a very sharp knife, remove all the skin and white pith from each of the oranges and the grapefruit, remove any pips then blend the flesh to a mush in a food processor – you should end up with about 250ml/9fl oz in total so that you have the same amount as the sugar.

Warm over gentle heat, stirring, until the sugar has dissolved, then bring the pan to the boil. Lower the heat again and simmer gently for 20 minutes until reduced and slightly sticky. Remove from the heat, add the whiskey, and leave to stand for about 15 minutes before potting into sterilised jam or Kilner jars (page 144). Otherwise transfer to a bowl, cover with cling film and chill until needed. It will keep happily like this for up to one month in the fridge.

WHITE SODA BREAD

THIS IS THE BREAD THAT IS TRADITIONALLY MADE AT HOME, WHEN UNEXPECTED GUESTS SHOW UP AND THERE'S NOTHING IN THE HOUSE. FOR TIMES LIKE THIS WHEN THE FRIDGE IS BARE OF BUTTERMILK, SOUR ORDINARY MILK WITH THE JUICE OF HALF A LEMON. I MAKE IT INTO SCONES BY ADDING A TEASPOON OF CASTER SUGAR AND BAKING AT THE HIGHER TEMPERATURE OF 220°C/450°F/GAS 7 FOR ABOUT 15 MINUTES.

450g/1lb/4 cups plain flour

1 tsp bicarbonate of soda

1 tsp salt

about 400ml/14fl oz/1 ¾ cups buttermilk

sunflower oil, for greasing

butter, to serve

Makes 1 loaf

Preheat the oven to 180°C/350°F/Gas 4. Mix the flour, bicarbonate of soda and salt in a bowl. Make a well in the centre. Pour in all of the buttermilk. Using a large spoon, gently and quickly stir the liquid into the flour. It should be soft but not sticky. Place in a 900g/2lb well oiled loaf tin and bake for 60 minutes. Run a knife around the tin and ease the bread out. If it sounds hollow when tapped on the bottom it is cooked; if not return it to the oven for another 5-10 minutes. There's no need to put the loaf back in the tin; turn it upside down and put it directly on the shelf. Transfer to a wire rack to cool.

TO SERVE, eat within hours, cut into slices with butter or freeze.

BROWN SODA BREAD For a light, brown mix use about three-quarters plain flour with one-quarter coarse stoneground wholemeal and add one to two tablespoons of pinhead oatmeal or very finely chopped nuts or seeds to the mix before adding the buttermilk. You can also experiment by adding a handful of bran or wheatgerm or both, just be prepared to slightly increase the quantity of buttermilk.

DUNBRODY RASPBERRY JAM

THE END RESULT IS A RICHLY FLAVOURED JAM WHICH IS DELICIOUS ON SCONES (SEE INTRODUCTION ABOVE) PILED WITH CREAM, AS THE FILLING OF A SPONGE FLAN CASE, TOPPED WITH WHIPPED CREAM AND FRESH FRUIT, OR MELTED GENTLY, SEASONED WITH A SLURP OF BRANDY AND USED AS A SAUCE FOR A SUMMER PUDDING. TRY IT AS A FILLING FOR PANCAKES, TOO.

1kg/2 ¼ lb raspberries, fresh or frozen

1kg/2 ¼ lb/4 ½ cups sugar

Makes about 1 litre/1 ¾ pints/4 ½ cups

Place the raspberries and sugar in a large heavy-based pan. Crush the berries lightly and cook on a gentle heat, stirring, until the sugar dissolves. Bring to the boil, then boil fast for 15 minutes, stirring occasionally and skimming off any rising foam with a spoon. Continue to boil for another 30 minutes or so until a small amount sets on a chilled saucer, when cool.

Remove from the heat and let it stand for about 15 minutes before potting into sterilised jam or Kilner jars (page 144). Otherwise transfer to a bowl, cover with cling film and chill until needed. It will keep happily like this for up to one month in the fridge.

ONION MARMALADE

THIS IS ONE OF MY STORE-CUPBOARD ESSENTIALS THAT'S SIMPLE TO MAKE AND STREETS AHEAD OF ANYTHING YOU CAN BUY. IT HAS SO MANY DIFFERENT USES. TRY IT IN SANDWICHES OR STIRRED INTO CREAMY MASHED POTATOES, OR SERVE WITH COLD MEATS OR MY COUNTRY PATÉ (PAGE 79). I SOMETIMES USE IT AS THE BASE FOR A TART. SPREAD A FEW TABLESPOONFULS OVER A CIRCLE OF PUFF PASTRY AND TOP WITH SLICES OF GOAT'S CHEESE. SERVE WITH A LIGHTLY DRESSED ROCKET SALAD FOR AN APPETIZER OR LIGHT LUNCH.

4 red onions, thinly sliced

50g/2oz/ ¼ cup sugar

50ml/2fl oz/ ¼ cup red wine vinegar

50ml/2fl oz/ ¼ cup red wine

dash grenadine syrup

Makes about 300ml/ ½ pint/1 ⅓ cups

Place the onions and sugar in a heavy-based pan and cook over a gentle heat for 10-15 minutes until the onions have softened and the sugar has completely dissolved, stirring regularly.

Stir the red wine vinegar and wine into the onion and sugar mixture. Bring to the boil, then reduce the heat and simmer for another 5 minutes until the marmalade is well thickened and slightly sticky. All the liquid should be just about gone. Add the grenadine and mix well, then leave to cool completely.

If you are not planning on using the onion marmalade immediately, sterilise a Kilner jar or a couple of jam jars (page 144). Otherwise transfer to a bowl, cover with cling film and chill until needed. It will keep happily like this for up to one week in the fridge.

HERB OIL

THIS IS OBVIOUSLY THE PERFECT OIL TO DRIZZLE OVER A TOMATO SALAD OR A PLATE OF WARM PASTA, BUT IT IS ALSO VERY GOOD TO USE FOR THE INITIAL SWEATING OF ONIONS FOR A TOMATO SOUP OR SAUCE. ALTERNATIVELY, USE IT TO GARNISH PLATES OR SOUPS AND LET YOUR GUESTS INHALE THE SCENT BEFORE THEY EAT. I FIND IT BEST TO MAKE THIS IN SMALL QUANTITIES AND AIM TO USE IT WITHIN THREE MONTHS.

100g/4oz fresh basil sprigs

150ml/ ¼ pint/ ⅔ cup olive oil

Makes 150ml/ ¼ pint/ ⅔ cup

Pick the leaves from the basil and then blanch them in a large pan of boiling water for 1 minute. Drain in a sieve and then rinse under cold running water to prevent them from cooking any further. Squeeze off any excess water and then tip on to kitchen paper and pat dry.

Place the blanched basil leaves into a food processor or liquidiser with the olive oil and blitz to a very fine purée, scraping down the sides of the container once or twice. Pass the purée through the sieve set over a jug or bowl, pressing down with the back of a ladle or wooden spoon until all of the liquid has gone through the sieve. Pour the herb oil into a squeezy bottle and leave to settle for at least 30 minutes to clear before using as required. Store in a cool place.

APRICOT CHUTNEY

THE PRONOUNCED FLAVOUR OF DRIED APRICOTS MAKES A RICH TASTING CHUTNEY WITH THE MINIMUM OF EFFORT. IT IS NOT AT ALL SEASONAL SO IT'S PERFECT FOR MAKING AT ANY TIME OF THE YEAR. I FIND THAT IT GOES PARTICULARLY WELL WITH MY COUNTRY PATÉ (PAGE 79), OR ANY COLD MEATS OR AS PART OF A CHEESE BOARD. IT CAN ALSO ACCOMPANY MILDLY CURRIED DISHES WITH GREAT SUCCESS. TRY IN A SANDWICH WITH HAND-CARVED HAM AND A HANDFUL OF SHREDDED LETTUCE FOR SOME EXTRA CRUNCH, IN BUTTERED GRANARY BREAD.

450g/1lb ready-to-eat apricots, cut into strips

200g/7oz raisins

1 onion, finely chopped

375g/13oz/1¾ cups light muscovado sugar

375ml/13fl oz/1½ cups white wine vinegar

1 tsp salt

Makes about 1.5kg/3lb

Place the apricots in a heavy-based pan with the raisins, onion, sugar, vinegar and salt. Bring to the boil over a moderate heat, stirring until the sugar has dissolved. Turn the heat down to a gentle simmer and cook for about 30 minutes until well reduced and syrupy, stirring frequently. Remove from the heat and leave to cool completely.

If you are not planning on using the apricot chutney immediately, sterilise a Kilner jar or a couple of jam jars (page 144). Otherwise transfer to a bowl, cover with cling film and chill until needed. It will keep happily like this for up to one month in the fridge.

OVEN DRIED TOMATOES

THESE ARE A SWEET AND PLUMP VERSION OF WHAT USUALLY COMES IN JARS LABELLED SUN-DRIED TOMATOES AND WHICH, IN MY OPINION CAN OFTEN TASTE DISAPPOINTING. THIS RECIPE SHOWS HOW TO MAKE THEM YOURSELF BUT BEWARE! IT IS IMPORTANT TO GET GOOD, RIPE PLUM TOMATOES: THE LITTLE DUTCH WATERBALLS JUST WON'T WORK. I OFTEN PUT THEM INTO THE OVEN FOR THE LAST HOUR WITH THE SUNDAY ROAST. THE FLAVOUR OF THE MEAT INFUSES INTO THE TOMATOES IMPARTING A WONDERFUL SAVOURY TASTE. USE WITH GREAT EFFECT ON TOP OF PIZZAS, OR IN SALADS. FOR AN ALMOST INSTANT PASTA SAUCE, SAUTÉ SLICED GARLIC CLOVES IN A GLUG OF OLIVE OIL AND ADD IN THE OVEN DRIED TOMATOES WITH SOME CHOPPED COOKED HAM. FINISH WITH A SCATTERING OF PARMESAN SHAVINGS AND A DRIBBLE OF MY HERB OIL (PAGE 158).

50g/2oz rock sea salt

handful fresh basil leaves

6 ripe plum tomatoes

about 200ml/7fl oz/1 scant cup olive oil

Fills a 500ml/18fl oz Kilner jar, or 2¼ cups

Sprinkle an even layer of sea salt and basil leaves on a baking sheet. Cut the tomatoes in half and arrange on top, cut side up. Bake for 50 minutes to 1 hour until slightly shrunk and then leave to cool completely.

Transfer the oven dried tomatoes to a sterilised Kilner jar (page 144), discarding the sea salt and basil leaves and pour over enough olive oil to cover the tomatoes completely. Otherwise transfer to a bowl, cover with cling film and chill until needed. these will keep happily like this for up to two weeks in the fridge.

CHILLI JAM

MY KITCHEN IS NEVER WITHOUT A BOWL OF THIS. IT IS AN IDEAL SUBSTITUTE IN RECIPES FOR SHOP-BOUGHT SWEET CHILLI SAUCE. I USE IT AS A DIPPING SAUCE FOR SPRING ROLLS, WONTONS AND TEMPURA OR TO DRIZZLE ON TO THE PLATES OF ORIENTAL DISHES. ADD A TABLESPOON TO YOUR FAVOURITE STIR FRY OR BRUSH ON TO FIRM WHITE FISH FILLETS BEFORE GRILLING FOR A FANTASTIC GLAZE.

2 mild red chillies, seeded and cut into julienne (long thin strips)

200g/7oz/1 scant cup caster sugar

225ml/8fl oz/1 cup white wine vinegar

Makes about 225ml/8fl oz/1 cup

Place the chillies in a pan with the sugar and vinegar and bring to the boil over a moderate heat, stirring until the sugar has dissolved. Reduce the heat and simmer for about 10 minutes or until reduced by half. Remove from the heat and leave to cool completely, then transfer to a bowl and cover with cling film. Place in the fridge and use as required. It will keep for up to six months.

CLARIFIED BUTTER

CLARIFIED BUTTER IS JUST THE OILY PART OF BUTTER, WITHOUT THE BUTTERMILK. YOU CAN BUY IT READY PREPARED IN ETHNIC STORES UNDER THE NAME GHEE. IF YOU HAVE A MICROWAVE, PUT THE BUTTER IN A PLASTIC JUG AND MICROWAVE ON A HIGH HEAT FOR 1 MINUTE. IF IT IS NOT COMPLETELY MELTED, GIVE IT ANOTHER 30 SECONDS. DO NOT ALLOW IT TO BOIL. CONTINUE AS DESCRIBED BELOW.

250g/9oz packet butter (2 ½ sticks)

Makes about 200ml/7fl oz

Melt the butter in a small pan over a low heat. Leave to stand for a few minutes until all the oil rises to the top, then skim off the oil into a sealable plastic container. It will keep for two months in the fridge.

BALSAMIC REDUCTION

THIS INTENSIFIES THE FLAVOUR OF THE VINEGAR AND ALSO MAKES IT THICK AND SYRUPY SO IT LOOKS GREAT WHEN DRIZZLED ON TO A PLATE, ESPECIALLY ALONG WITH MY HERB OIL (PAGE 158). IT IS EXCELLENT DRIZZLED OVER ROASTED MEDITERRANEAN VEGETABLES, PARMA HAM, SALAD, ROCKET OR ANYTHING ITALIAN FOR THAT MATTER. TRY ROASTING RAW BEETROOT WEDGES IN A GLUG WITH THE SAME QUANTITY OF OLIVE OIL AND SERVING THEM WITH A DOLLOP OF HORSERADISH CREAM (PAGE 91).

500ml/18fl oz bottle, or 2 ¼ cups balsamic vinegar

200g/7oz/1 scant cup sugar

Makes about 300ml/ ½ pint/1 ⅓ cups

Place the balsamic vinegar and sugar in a heavy-based pan and bring to the boil over a moderate heat, stirring until the sugar had dissolved. Reduce the heat and simmer for about 10 minutes or until reduced by half. It should be thick and syrupy. We store ours in small squeezy bottles for convenience. It will keep for up to six months in a cool, dark place.

BALSAMIC VINAIGRETTE

THIS WILL KEEP HAPPILY IN THE FRIDGE FOR UP TO ONE MONTH. IT TAKES JUST MINUTES TO MAKE AND IS FAR SUPERIOR TO ANY SHOP-BOUGHT ALTERNATIVES. YOU CAN ADAPT THIS VINAIGRETTE TO YOUR OWN TASTES BY USING RED OR WHITE WINE VINEGAR, OR EXPERIMENT WITH DIFFERENT OILS.

50ml/2fl oz/ ¼ cup balsamic vinegar (preferably 9 year old toschi)

150ml/ ¼ pint/ ⅔ cup olive oil

2 tsp Dijon mustard

salt and freshly ground black pepper

Makes about 175ml/6fl oz/ ¾ cup

Place the balsamic vinegar in a screw-topped jar, add a good pinch of salt and shake until the salt has dissolved.

Add the olive oil to the jar with the mustard and shake again until you have formed a thick emulsion. Season to taste and chill until needed.

RASPBERRY VINAIGRETTE Replace the balsamic vinegar with raspberry vinegar and omit the mustard.

DALKEY MUSTARD DRESSING

juice of ½ lemon

pinch caster sugar

6 tbsp/7 ½ US tablespoons olive oil

1 tbsp/1 ¼ US tablespoons wholegrain mustard

salt and freshly ground black pepper

Makes about 100ml/3 ½ fl oz/ ½ cup

THE NAME OF THIS DRESSING DERIVES FROM MY FAVOURITE WHOLEGRAIN MUSTARD THAT IS CALLED AFTER A SUBURB IN DUBLIN, DALKEY. THIS CAN ALSO BE MADE IN A BOWL WITH A WHISK BUT I FIND A CLEAN JAM JAR EXCELLENT FOR STORAGE.

Place the lemon juice in a screw-topped jar, add the sugar and a good pinch of salt, then shake until the salt has dissolved.

Add the oil to the jar with the mustard and shake again until you have formed a thick emulsion. Season to taste and chill until needed.

MIXED BERRY COMPÔTE

IF YOU ARE MAKING THIS IN THE RIGHT SEASON, YOU MIGHT LIKE TO USE A MIXTURE OF SUMMER BERRIES OTHERWISE, THE CARTONS OF FROZEN MIXED BERRIES WORK BRILLIANTLY. THIS IS A VERY VERSATILE RECIPE, USEFUL FOR BOTH SAVOURY AND SWEET DISHES. SERVE VERY COLD WITH CRÈME FRAÎCHE FOR AN INSTANT DESSERT, OR FOLD INTO SORBETS OR ICE CREAM OR USE TO FILL MERINGUES WITH LASHINGS OF WHIPPED CREAM. IT IS USED WITH GREAT EFFECT IN MY SPECTACULAR ORANGE SCENTED PASTRY CAGE WITH FRESH BERRIES AND GRAND MARNIER ICE CREAM (PAGE 129). I ALSO LIKE TO SERVE A SPOONFUL WITH SOME MILD CREAMY GOAT'S CHEESE AND A COUPLE OF CROSTINI AS AN INSTANT STARTER.

200g/7oz mixed berries, such as blueberries, raspberries, blackberries hulled and halved strawberries

50g/2oz/4 US tablespoons sugar

2 tbsp/2 ½ US tablespoons Grand Marnier

Makes about 300ml/ ½ pint

Place the berries in a heavy-based pan with the sugar and Grand Marnier, then stir over a gentle heat to dissolve the sugar. Increase the heat and boil fast for about 5 minutes until the berries are tender but still holding their shape.

Remove the compôte from the heat and transfer to a bowl. Leave to cool completely, then cover with cling film and chill until needed. This will last for up to three days in the fridge.

BUTTERSCOTCH SAUCE

THIS BUTTERSCOTCH SAUCE IS MOST OF THE MOST INVALUABLE THINGS IN THE RESTAURANT KITCHEN. SERVE WITH ICE CREAM OR AS A DIP FOR FRESH FRUIT. I LIKE TO SPREAD IT OVER A CHEESECAKE BASE AND THEN COVER WITH SLICED BANANAS AND PILE ON LIGHTLY WHIPPED CREAM BEFORE DRIZZLING WITH A LITTLE MELTED CHOCOLATE FOR AN INSTANT BANOFFI PIE.

50g/2oz/ ½ stick unsalted butter

50g/2oz/4 US tablespoons light muscovado sugar

2 tbsp/2 ½ US tablespoons pouring golden syrup or clear honey

2 tbsp/2 ½ US tablespoons double cream

Makes about 200ml/7fl oz/1 scant cup

Place the butter in a small pan with the sugar and golden syrup or honey. Bring to the boil over a moderate heat, stirring until the sugar has dissolved. Reduce the heat, then add the cream and simmer for 2-3 minutes until thickened. Remove from the heat and use immediately or transfer to a bowl and leave to cool completely. If keeping for any length of time, up to one week is fine, cover with cling film and store in the fridge.

EGG CUSTARD

IF YOU ARE NERVOUS OF CURDLING THE CUSTARD BEAT TWO TEASPOONS OF CORNFLOUR IN WITH THE EGG YOLKS, WHICH WILL HELP THICKEN AND STABILISE THE SAUCE. JUST MAKE SURE THAT YOU TASTE IT AFTER COOKING TO ENSURE THAT THE TASTE OF CORNFLOUR HAS DISAPPEARED; IF NECESSARY, STIR OVER A GENTLE HEAT FOR A LITTLE LONGER, BUT DO NOT BOIL.

600ml/1 pint/2 ¾ cups milk

6 egg yolks

3 tbsp/3 ¾ US tablespoons caster sugar

few drops vanilla extract or ½ vanilla pod, split and seeds scraped out

Makes about 700ml/1 ¼ pint/3 cups

Bring the milk to scalding point in a non-stick pan. Meanwhile, place the egg yolks in a bowl with the sugar and vanilla, stirring to combine. Gradually whisk the hot milk into the egg yolk mixture.

Wipe out the pan and pour in the egg mixture, then cook, stirring constantly, over a gentle heat for about 10 minutes until the custard thickens. Do not let it boil or it will curdle and watch out for the froth: when it begins to disappear from the surface, the custard is starting to thicken. Pour into a serving jug and serve at once or leave to cool, then cover with cling film and store in the fridge covered with cling film for up to two days.

CARAMEL

MAKE SURE THAT YOU WAIT UNTIL THE SUGAR HAS COMPLETELY DISSOLVED BEFORE BOILING THE LIQUID, AND NEVER STIR ONCE THE SYRUP BOILS. FOR A DRAMATIC EFFECT, PLACE CHUNKS OF FRESH FRUIT IN THE BOTTOM OF A GLASS SERVING DISH. COVER WITH A MIXTURE OF LIGHTLY WHIPPED CREAM AND CRÈME FRAÎCHE, THEN CHILL FOR AT LEAST TWO HOURS UNTIL REALLY COLD. TO SERVE, POUR OVER THE HOT CARAMEL AND WATCH IT BUBBLE AND SET BEFORE YOUR EYES!

100g/4oz/scant ½ cup caster sugar

Makes about 100ml/3 ½ fl oz/ scant ½ cup

Place the caster sugar in a heavy-based pan over a low heat and heat gently to dissolve. Bring to the boil and boil fast until the resulting syrup begins to turn pale brown, gently swirling the pan to ensure even cooking. When the caramel is rich golden brown, dip the base of the pan into a sink of cool water to prevent further cooking.

SPUN-SUGAR CORKSCREWS Using a clean, small metal spoon and knife-sharpening steel, dip the spoon into the caramel and lift it out again, then twist it around the steel to create some corkscrews. Use within 1 hour for decoration.

SPUN-SUGAR DISCS Drizzle the caramel in small zig-zag patterns on to a baking sheet lined with non-stick parchment paper. Leave to set and use within an hour for decoration.

CARAMEL SHARDS Pour the caramel into a non-stick shallow tin and leave to set. Break into shards with a rolling pin and sprinkle over desserts or bowls of ice cream.

CHOCOLATE CURLS

THESE CHOCOLATE CURLS CAN BE SPRINKLED OVER ALMOST ANY CHOCOLATE DESSERT FOR A DELICATE FINISHING TOUCH. THE TWO MAIN THINGS TO REMEMBER WHEN MELTING CHOCOLATE ARE TO MELT IT SLOWLY AND NEVER LET IT GET TOO HOT.

100g/4oz plain chocolate (at least 50% cocoa solids)

Makes 8–12 chocolate curls

Place 75g/3oz of the chocolate in a heatproof bowl set over a pan of simmering water and heat gently until the chocolate has melted. Remove from the heat and stir in the remaining 25g/1oz of the chocolate. Continue to stir until the chocolate is smooth and glossy. This will help temper the chocolate.

Pour the chocolate on to a very cold marble slab and allow to set at room temperature. If you put it in the fridge the chocolate will loose its wonderful sheen. Using a large sharp knife, pare long curls off the surface of the hardened chocolate, carefully adjusting the angle of the knife as you work. Use as required.

SUGAR PASTRY

THERE ARE A MULTITUDE OF FILLINGS YOU CAN USE WITH THIS. LET YOUR IMAGINATION RUN WILD. AS THE PASTRY IS SO SHORT, IT IS VERY DIFFICULT TO ROLL OUT SO YOU MAY FIND IT MUCH EASIER TO PRESS INTO THE TARTLET TINS FOR A SEAMLESS FINISH.

150g/5oz /1½ sticks butter, softened

150g/5oz/1 cup plus 2 US tablespoons icing sugar, sifted

2 egg yolks, beaten

1 tbsp/1¼ US tablespoons cream

300g/11oz/2⅓ cups plain flour, sifted plus extra for dusting

Makes about 600 g/1 lb 6 oz

To make the pastry, gently cream the butter and sugar in a bowl until pale and fluffy. Slowly add the egg yolks, mixing well after each addition. Stir in the cream and then tip in the flour and mix to a smooth paste. Cover with cling film and leave to rest for at least 4 hours or overnight is best in the fridge. Use as required or freeze down into portions.

To use, leave to thaw at room temperature for 2 hours or overnight in the fridge. Use plenty of flour to roll the pastry out on the work surface and when lining tins join any breakages using the tips of your fingers for a seamless result.

THE LARDER

VANILLA ICE CREAM

I ALWAYS USE THE SAME BASIC RECIPE FOR VANILLA ICE CREAM, BUT ALTERNATIVE FLAVOURS ALSO WORK BRILLIANTLY. FOR MOST RECIPES THE VANILLA CAN BE LEFT OUT SO THAT THE OTHER FLAVOURS CAN PREDOMINATE. IF YOU HAVEN'T GOT AN ICE CREAM MACHINE, THEN PUT THE VANILLA MIXTURE INTO A BOWL AND FREEZE, TURNING WITH A WHISK EVERY 15 MINUTES UNTIL FROZEN.

150g/5oz/ ¾ cup sugar

600ml/1 pint/2 ¾ cups cream

5 egg yolks

1 vanilla pod, split and seeds scraped out or 1 tsp vanilla extract

2 tbsp/2 ½ US tablespoons hand-hot water

Makes about 900ml/1 ½ pints/1 quart

Place the sugar in a heavy-based pan with 120ml/4fl oz/½ cup of water. Place over a low heat and heat gently until the sugar has dissolved. Bring to the boil and boil fast for a few minutes until the resulting syrup begins to reach soft ball stage. Test by quickly dipping the back of two spoons into the syrup, if it strings between them then it is ready.

Place the cream in a large bowl and beat until soft peaks form. Whip the egg yolks and vanilla in a separate bowl with the hand-hot water until pale and thickened and the whisk can leave a trail in the mixture. Slowly pour in the sugar syrup and then fold into the whipped cream.

Place the vanilla mixture into an ice cream maker and churn for 20-30 minutes until thickened and increased in volume. Don't leave it churning until completely frozen and set or it will be over-churned and slightly grainy in texture. Take it out when thick and starting to freeze and put into the freezer. Ice cream is best served within 24 hours. Transfer it to the fridge for 30 minutes before serving to soften a little.

MIXED BERRY ICE CREAM Add the Mixed berry compôte (page 162) at the last turn or two. This will give you a wonderful ripple effect running through the ice cream.

GRAND MARNIER Fold four tablespoons of Grand Marnier into the ice cream mixture before churning.

BROWN BREAD Preheat the oven to 180°C/350°F/Gas 4. Spread 75g/3oz of Brown soda bread crumbs (page 157) on a baking sheet and sprinkle over the same amount of light muscovado sugar. Bake for 10-15 minutes until the crumbs are toasted and lightly caramelised, stirring occasionally to break up any lumps. Remove from the oven and leave to cool completely, then using your fingers separate into fine crumbs and add at the last turn or two to keep the crunchy texture.

THYME INFUSED CHICKEN STOCK

WHILE THIS STOCK DOES TAKE A BIT OF TIME TO MAKE, YOU CAN, OF COURSE, STORE IT IN THE FREEZER FOR FUTURE USE. IF YOU'D LIKE A STRONGER FLAVOURED JELLIED STOCK, RETURN THE STRAINED STOCK TO A CLEAN PAN AND BOIL UNTIL REDUCED BY HALF. I WOULD THEN FREEZE THIS IN ICE CUBE TRAYS AND TRANSFER TO FREEZER BAGS FOR STORAGE. USE STRAIGHT FROM THE FREEZER FOR SAUCES.

2kg/4½ lb bony chicken wings or raw carcasses, roughly chopped

3 large fresh thyme sprigs

2 onions, roughly chopped

2 leeks, roughly chopped

3 celery sticks, roughly chopped

2 carrots, roughly chopped

½ head garlic (unpeeled)

2 tsp Maldon sea salt

Makes about 2 litres/3 ½ pints/ 2 quarts plus 1 cup

Preheat the oven to 200°C/400°F/Gas 6. Place the chicken wings or carcasses into a large roasting tin and roast for 15-20 minutes, turning them over once or twice until dark golden in colour.

Place the roasted chicken bones in a stockpot or large pan with the thyme. Pour over 4 litres/7 pints/4½ quarts of water and bring to the boil, skimming off any scum from the surface with a spoon.

Add the onions, leeks, celery and carrots to the pan with the garlic and salt. Return to the boil, then reduce the heat and simmer, uncovered for about 3 hours, skimming occasionally.

Taste the stock to check the flavour and when you are happy with it, remove from the heat and strain through a muslin-lined colander into a large jug or bowl, discarding the bones, vegetables and herbs. Leave to cool, cover with cling film and place in the fridge. Use within three days, or freeze into 500ml/18fl oz/2¼ cups sealable plastic containers and use within a month.

FENNEL SCENTED FISH STOCK

FOR A MORE CONCENTRATED FISH FLAVOUR TO USE AS THE BASIS FOR SAUCES, REDUCE THE STRAINED STOCK BY HALF AGAIN AND FREEZE IN ICE CUBE TRAYS. TRANSFER TO FREEZER BAGS FOR STORAGE.

1 onion, chopped

1 leek, chopped

1 celery stick, chopped

2 garlic cloves, not peeled

100ml/3½ fl oz/scant ½ cup olive oil

1.5kg/3lb white fish bones and head, well rinsed and roughly chopped

300ml/½ pint/1⅓ cups white wine

2 each fresh flat-leaf parsley and thyme sprigs tied together with string

½ lemon, sliced

¼ tsp white peppercorns

3 fresh fennel sprigs

Makes about 2 litres/3 ½ pints/ 2 quarts plus 1 cup

Place the onion, leek, celery and garlic in a large stockpot or large pan with a lid. Add the oil and heat until the vegetables start to sizzle. Cover and gently sweat the vegetables over a low heat for about 15 minutes until softened but not coloured.

Stir the fish bones and head into the pan with the wine and cook until almost all of the liquid has evaporated. Pour in 2 litres/3½ pints/2 quarts plus 1 cup of water with the herbs, lemon and peppercorns. Bring to the boil, skimming off the scum from the surface with a spoon.

Reduce the heat and simmer, uncovered for 20 minutes, no longer or the bones will become bitter. Remove from the heat, stir in the fennel sprigs and set aside for 10 minutes to allow the flavours to infuse.

Line a large colander with wet muslin and set over a large jug or bowl. Carefully strain through the liquid, discarding the bones, vegetables and herbs. Leave to cool, cover with cling film and place in the fridge. Use within three days, or freeze into 500ml/18fl oz/2¼ cups sealable plastic containers and use within a month.

KITCHEN GARDEN VEGETABLE STOCK

I LIKE TO MARINATE THIS FOR 24 HOURS FOR AN INTENSE FLAVOUR. WHEN CUTTING GARLIC FOR STOCK, ALWAYS CUT THE GARLIC HEADS ACROSS THEIR 'EQUATORS'. THIS GIVES YOU SOLELY THE SWEET GARLIC FLAVOURS AND NOT THE HARSH GARLIC OIL.

3 onions, roughly chopped

1 leek, roughly chopped

2 celery sticks, roughly chopped

6 carrots, roughly chopped

½ head garlic, (unpeeled)

¼ tsp white peppercorns

¼ tsp pink peppercorns

1 small bay leaf

1 fresh sprig each of basil, coriander, thyme, parsley, chervil and tarragon, tied together with string

200ml/7fl oz/1 scant cup white wine

Makes about 2 litres/3 ½ pints/2 quarts plus 1 cup

Place the onions, leek, celery, carrots and garlic in a stock-pot or large pan. Add the peppercorns and herbs. Pour in 2 litres/3 ½ pints/2 quarts plus 1 cup of water and bring to the boil. Reduce the heat and simmer for 10 minutes.

Remove from the heat and stir in the wine, then push the herbs right down into the liquid and set aside to cool completely. When the stock is cold, transfer to a large jug or bowl. Cover with cling film and chill for 24 hours.

The next day, strain the stock through a muslin-lined colander into a clean jug or bowl, discarding the vegetables, peppercorns and herbs. Cover with cling film and place in the fridge. Use within three days, or freeze into 500ml/ 18fl oz/2 ¼ cups sealable plastic containers and use within a month.

Dinner Parties

Dinner Parties

SPRING

SUMMER

AUTUMN

WINTER

SMOKED SALMON CAKE WITH CHIVE CREAM CHEESE
page 40

OVEN BAKED POUSSIN WITH SAGE AND ROASTED GARLIC
page 95

MUM'S ROAST POTATOES
page 140

BRAISED FENNEL
page 142

HONEY-GLAZED CARROTS
page 145

IRISH WHISKEY CHOCOLATE FONDANT
page 125

US CONVERSIONS

100g/4oz butter = 1 stick

225ml/8fl oz liquid = 1 cup

225g/8oz sugar = 1 cup

115g/4oz flour, firmly packed = 1 cup

1 US tablespoon = 14.2ml

1 UK/Irish tablespoon = 17.7ml

FREQENTLY USED EUROPEAN/US TERMS

aubergine : eggplant

bicarbonate of soda : baking soda

coriander : cilantro

cornflour : cornstarch

cling film : plastic wrap

caster sugar : superfine sugar

icing sugar : powdered or confectioner's sugar

muscovado sugar : unrefined sugar

plain flour : all-purpose flour

red and green peppers : red and green bell peppers

rocket : arugula

spring onions : scallions

treacle : molasses

wholemeal flour : wholewheat flour